A 40-DAY EXPERIENCE
TO ACTIVATE YOUR FAITH

SUN STAND STILL

DEVOTIONAL

STEVEN FURTICK

NEW YORK TIMES BEST-SELLING AUTHOR

with Eric Stanford

MULTNOMAH
BOOKS

SUN STAND STILL DEVOTIONAL
PUBLISHED BY MULTNOMAH BOOKS
12265 Oracle Boulevard, Suite 200
Colorado Springs, Colorado 80921

All Scripture quotations, unless otherwise indicated, are taken from the Holy Bible, New International Version®, NIV®. Copyright © 1973, 1978, 1984 by Biblica Inc.™ Used by permission of Zondervan. All rights reserved worldwide. www.zondervan.com. Scripture quotations marked (KJV) are taken from the King James Version. Scripture quotations marked (NKJV) are taken from the New King James Version®. Copyright © 1982 by Thomas Nelson Inc. Used by permission. All rights reserved.

Italics in Scripture quotations reflect the author's added emphasis.

Details in some anecdotes and stories have been changed to protect the identities of the persons involved.

Hardcover ISBN 978-1-60142-523-2
eBook ISBN 978-1-60142-524-9

Content in this book is drawn from *Sun Stand Still,* copyright 2010 by Steven Furtick, published by Multnomah Books, and other published and unpublished works by Steven Furtick.

Cover design by Ryan Hollingsworth

Published in the United States by WaterBrook Multnomah, an imprint of the Crown Publishing Group, a division of Random House LLC, New York, a Penguin Random House Company.

MULTNOMAH and its mountain colophon are registered trademarks of Random House LLC.

Library of Congress Cataloging-in-Publication Data
 Furtick, Steven.
   Sun stand still devotional : a forty-day experience to activate your faith / Steven Furtick.
     pages cm
   ISBN 978-1-60142-523-2 (hardback)— ISBN 978-1-60142-524-9 (electronic)
 1. Prayer—Christianity—Meditations. 2. Christian life—Prayers and devotions.
 3. Faith—Prayers and devotions. 4. Bible. Joshua, X, 12-13—Devotional literature.
 I. Title.
   BV220.F8723 2013
   242—dc23

                                                 2013029576

Printed in the United States of America
2013—First Edition

10 9 8 7 6 5 4 3 2 1

SPECIAL SALES
Most WaterBrook Multnomah books are available at special quantity discounts when purchased in bulk by corporations, organizations, and special-interest groups. Custom imprinting or excerpting can also be done to fit special needs. For information, please e-mail SpecialMarkets@WaterBrookMultnomah.com or call 1-800-603-7051.

The Cure for the Ache of the Ordinary

Thank you for picking up this copy of the *Sun Stand Still Devotional*. Whoever you are, whatever you're going through, I pray God will use it to elevate your life to a new level.

This book provides forty daily readings paired with powerful Bible passages and targeted prayer suggestions for use in your quiet time with God. The daily readings are based on my book *Sun Stand Still* and on other things I've written or preached on the topic of audacious faith. They are designed to help you become someone who dares to believe God for the impossible.

In *Sun Stand Still* I retell the biblical story of Joshua, who—in the middle of a battle—threw out one of the most amazing prayers recorded in the Bible. With sunset approaching and Israel's enemies on the run, he actually asked God to stop the sun and moon, to extend the day, so Israel could complete its victory. Most people would never even think of praying a prayer like that. Yet Joshua not only thought it; he prayed it. And even more amazing—God did it.

"The sun stopped in the middle of the sky," we're told, "and delayed going down about a full day. There has never been a day like it before or since, a day when the LORD listened to a man" (Joshua 10:13–14).

That's audacious faith.

That's the impossible made actual.

And what I suggest in the book is, why can't it happen again? Why can't we have faith like Joshua's? And why can't the very same God who made the sun stand still in the sky for Joshua do equally incredible things for us?

I've seen God answer Sun Stand Still prayers many times in my own life. He's still doing it. And more than that, over and over again people have come up to me to tell me about the amazing things God is doing in their lives in response to their bold prayers. I never get tired of hearing these stories.

Of course, the reality is that most of us don't go from ordinary faith to audacious faith overnight. Audacious faith normally has to be formed within us over time.

And that's where the *Sun Stand Still Devotional* comes in.

If you're feeling what I call "the ache of the ordinary"—discouraged because your life of faith in Jesus seems like nothing much—then let this book of short readings become a tool God can use to transform the ordinary into the extraordinary in your life. In the *Sun Stand Still Devotional,* you will learn more about our miracle-working God through His Word, submit yourself daily to Him in prayer for the changes He wants to make, and develop an audacious faith of your own.

There's a move of God under way, and all of Jesus's followers are supposed to be a part of it. His work in our world and in our lives is always far beyond what we can do on our own. But that's only half the truth. The other half is this: with God's power unleashed in your life and mine through faith, the impossible *will* become possible.

The Prayer That Stopped the Sun

Joshua said to the LORD in the presence of Israel:
> *"O sun, stand still over Gibeon,*
>> *O moon, over the Valley of Aijalon."*
> *So the sun stood still,*
>> *and the moon stopped,*
>> *till the nation avenged itself on its enemies.*

—JOSHUA 10:12–13

Today's Bible reading: Joshua 10:1–14

Right here on Day 1, I'm going to throw out a challenge to you: If you're not daring to believe God for the impossible, you're sleeping through some of the best parts of your Christian life. And further still, if the size of your vision for your life isn't intimidating to you, there's a good chance it's insulting to God. You should be living by audacious faith every day. Audacity is not just for "elite Christians." It's intended for every believer. So today we're beginning a spiritual journey toward trusting God for what seems impossible. I'm thrilled to think about what it's going to do for our lives and our world.

A story from the life of Joshua serves as our template for audacious faith.

The Israelites unleash a surprise attack on the Amorites, and right from the beginning the battle goes well. But as the sun sinks toward the horizon, General Joshua faces a decision. The victory isn't complete, and once it gets dark, the rest of the Amorites will slip away. Joshua sizes up the situation and delivers one of the most gloriously unorthodox prayers in the Bible. He has the audacity to ask God to make the sun stop in the sky. To freeze time on behalf of His people.

And God gives Joshua exactly what he asked for.

With everything in me, I believe God still desires to make the sun stand still over the life of every believer. Obviously, not in the unique way He did for Joshua, but in ways that are equally spectacular (although not always quite as dramatic), God is perfectly willing to perform the impossible in our everyday lives. If we have the audacity to ask.

 RT God is ready to act if we will be bold enough to ask, not just for a good day or a better life, but for the impossible. #sunstandstill

---

I tried this one time.

My wife and I moved to Charlotte, North Carolina, with seven other families. We set a goal of reaching over one thousand people in our first year of ministry. Since the average church size in America is fewer than ninety, I guess we were overshooting a bit. But we wanted to see God accomplish something so exponentially amazing that it would leave no doubt who deserved the credit.

So we shamelessly asked God to exceed our wildest dreams.

The story of our church is still being written. But here's what I can tell you now. After seven years of ministry, our church has grown to more than twelve thousand people in regular attendance. Since our opening day, thousands of people have publicly professed faith in Christ.

Sometimes when we consider the rate at which God has multiplied this ministry, we feel like we're living in a warp-speed dream world. But the story is real. We are living in the middle of a move of God.

Is there something that is seemingly impossible that you'd like to see God do through you? Maybe God has already been working in your spirit, planting a desire, sparking ideas about the much bigger things He wants to accomplish.

There's nothing our world needs more desperately today—in individuals, families, businesses, churches, and communities—than God's saving, supernatural acts. And God is ready to act if we will be bold enough to ask, not just for a good day or a better life, but for the impossible and then will step forward to act in audacious faith.

PRAYER FOCUS: Over the next forty days, pray for God to build audacious faith within you and to show you where He wants you to apply it.

Your Page 23 Vision

*I have appeared to you to appoint you as a servant and
as a witness of what you have seen of me and what I
will show you.*

—ACTS 26:16

Today's Bible reading: Acts 26:1–23

Saul of Tarsus is going along on his religious way when one day
Jesus decides, *Enough of the ordinary religious order for this guy. I'm
going to demonstrate My grace to him in an extraordinary way.* I can
almost hear Jesus chuckling to Himself as He prepares His bolt of
lightning for the unsuspecting traveler.

Saul—nowadays better known as Paul—was never the same
after Jesus waylaid him on the road to Damascus. The world has
never been the same either. Because Jesus used Paul as a gospel
luminary to take the message of faith in Christ to the peoples of
the earth. "I am sending you to [the Gentiles]," Jesus told him,
"to open their eyes and turn them from darkness to light" (Acts
26:17–18).

God has a way of opening our eyes with a near-blinding epiphany when He's about to do something new through us.

A few months after my commitment to Christ at age sixteen, someone slipped me a book called *Fresh Wind, Fresh Fire*. Written by a pastor in Brooklyn named Jim Cymbala, it read like a highlight reel of the miracles God had performed in Cymbala's church. I was mesmerized.

 RT Accomplishing the impossible starts with seeing the invisible. #sunstandstill

---

As I sat at my parents' kitchen table with the open book, I stumbled across a line that set the trajectory of my life. It was on page 23: "I despaired at the thought that my life might slip by without seeing God show himself mightily on our behalf."

Somehow I knew: *One day I'm going to start a church in a big city to reach people far from God.*

The words in the Cymbala book set off a nuclear reaction in my soul. In retrospect I can identify it as an epiphany. At the time, though, it was just a strong impulse and a naive enthusiasm. I couldn't know what it would lead to. In fact, everything would change.

If it hasn't already happened to you, I believe *you* will have a Page 23 vision. A Damascus road moment. My prayer for you is that your epiphany happens very soon. It will start with a seed of inspiration that takes root in your imagination. Over time it will produce a harvest of obedience for the glory of God. And the whole process will take place deep in the soil of your faith.

To be clear, I'm not suggesting that the only visions God gives are about starting a church or doing the kinds of things we typically associate with ministry. In fact, in most cases there is no lightning bolt and no connection to a religious profession.

But the bottom line is this: if you're going to ask God to do something impossible in your life, you have to have some clarity about what you're asking for. You have to know you're not just spinning a fantasy or going on a delusional ego trip.

Meditate on this thought as you go through the day: *Accomplishing the impossible starts with seeing the invisible.*

PRAYER FOCUS: If you haven't already received a Page 23 vision, ask God to make you ready for it and receptive to it, sensitive to His word for you.

Ignite the Ordinary

God called to him from within the bush, "Moses! Moses!"

And Moses said, "Here I am."

"Do not come any closer," God said. "Take off your sandals, for the place where you are standing is holy ground."

—Exodus 3:4–5

Today's Bible reading: Exodus 3:1–10

When you strip the biblical miracles of their spectacular special effects, a common plot point emerges: extraordinary moves of God begin with ordinary acts of obedience.

Consider Moses's first encounter with God.

Moses is tending the family sheep out in the nondescript countryside.

He happens to notice a bush that's caught fire.

He walks over to take a look…

Up to this point, it's not exactly a riveting scene, is it?

In reality, the illustrious burning-bush encounter that seemed so captivating in Sunday school is…really…quite…ordinary. Moses is performing menial manual labor, working for his father-in-law. It's dusty. The sheep stink. Does it get any more mundane?

Almost all encounters with God begin that way. You may be living under the illusion that when God ignites great things in your life, He'll announce it with a big bang. He might. It's more likely that He won't. So stop waiting around for the big bang. Pay attention to the subtle clues and the still, small voice. Maybe you'll hear it this very day.

What we call a miracle is really just the right combination of your ordinary ingredients and God's extraordinary expertise. When God's super collides with your natural, sparks will fly.

God may call you to serve as an unknown youth pastor of fifteen kids in a moldy basement for a youth room and with an Atari for entertainment. Ordinary. But He may also be providing you an opportunity to pour your life into one of those teenagers who will go on to preach the gospel in a thousand places you'll never go. Extraordinary.

 RT When God's super collides with your natural, sparks will fly. #sunstandstill

---

God may lead you to stay at home with your young children, forfeiting a second income. Ordinary. But along with diapers, dishes, and naps, you receive the gift of time—to model discipline, instill values, and speak life into your kids. They could grow up to be Joshuas in their own generation. Extraordinary.

If God is calling you to make a big difference today, He is likely to start in a small way—a bush that only you will notice. Will you remove your shoes, draw close, and receive your assignment? Will you give the Lord permission to ignite your ordinary? If you will, before long your faith will start carrying you to a higher level than you ever thought you could reach.

PRAYER FOCUS: Ask God where your burning bush is. Tell Him you're ready to take off your sandals for a holy encounter with Him.

What Is Your Vision Worth to You?

I was very much afraid, but I said to the king, "May the king live forever! Why should my face not look sad when the city where my fathers are buried lies in ruins, and its gates have been destroyed by fire?"

—Nehemiah 2:2–3

Today's Bible reading: Nehemiah 2:1–10

This is not your normal vacation request to an employer. If Artaxerxes is displeased by what Nehemiah asks him for, he has the power to end Nehemiah's life. Gulp.

And even if Nehemiah gets what he wants—permission to go to Jerusalem and rebuild its walls—this will mean hardship. He will have to leave his comfortable job with the Persian government, travel across a desert, and undertake an immense project.

But Nehemiah has a vision for what God wants him to do. And this vision is worth everything to him.

When my wife and I and the other seven families on our team started Elevation Church, we all knew the costs would be relatively high. We sold our houses, quit our jobs, and moved to a different location. We had no salaries. No benefits. Just a burning conviction that there has to be more to life than 401(k)s, additional square footage, soccer leagues, and church as usual.

We had a vision. We knew it was from God. And it was worth everything we had to give up to watch it become a reality.

What is your vision for your life worth to you?

Here's how to know the answer to that question: What would you give up for your vision? Your time? Your pay grade? Your comfortable lifestyle? Your current career to start a new one? Your current home to move to a new one in a new city? Your relationships that are holding you back or bringing you down?

 RT If your vision for your life isn't worth giving yourself up for, it's not worth giving yourself to. #sunstandstill

---

Even your life?

If you wouldn't give up such things for it, the problem probably isn't that you're just not passionate enough about your vision. Now, it could be that—maybe you've somehow been lured into apathy and complacency about a vision that's truly worth everything—but probably not.

The problem more likely is that your vision isn't worth being passionate about. You've got the wrong vision. Or at least a vision that's too small.

Think about this today: if your vision for your life isn't worth giving yourself up for, it's not worth giving yourself to. Stop spinning your wheels over something that can't stir passion within you. Go back to the drawing board. Pray. Seek. Dream. And acquire a vision from God worthy of your life.

PRAYER FOCUS: Ask God to give you a vision for your life that's big enough to be passionate about. And the courage to take the risks needed to turn it into a reality.

Seize the Vision

*No one will be able to stand up against you all the
days of your life. As I was with Moses, so I will be
with you; I will never leave you nor forsake you.*

—JOSHUA 1:5

Today's Bible reading: Joshua 1:1–5

Most nights I slip into my boys' rooms after they're asleep, just
barely place my right hand on their heads, and whisper: "God,
raise up my sons to be the greatest men of God of their generation."
I tell them that I'm praying this for their lives when they're awake
too. Of course they don't understand many of the implications of
this. But one day they will. I'm just trying to stock their hearts with
raw material that God can use to build a vision within my boys
when they're older.

The point I'm trying to make has very little to do with me and
my boys. It has everything to do with you and your vision: If you
want to see God do something impossible in your life, you have to
open your heart and mind to God's vision for your life. You have
to seize it.

Joshua has been a faithful second in command for many years. But talk about having a tough act to follow. For the Hebrews, Moses was a legend in his own time—the president, chief justice, and chairman of the Joint Chiefs all rolled up in one. But now he is dead, and Joshua is next in line.

Joshua's term of office is starting at a perilous moment in the nation's history. The people are about to try to take Canaan from several people groups who aren't exactly eager to vacate the premises and hand it over.

 RT Stop trying to have all the answers before launching out in faith. #sunstandstill

---

The vision isn't in question: occupy the Promised Land. But before that can happen, Joshua has to seize the vision. And judging by the number of times "Be strong and courageous" shows up in Joshua 1, apparently God knows this leader is scared of failing.

God steps in with encouragement. Just as God was with Moses, so He will be with Joshua. God promises, "I will never leave you nor forsake you." (Interesting how He says the same thing to us [Hebrews 13:5, NKJV].)

Joshua seizes the vision. We know this because practically within moments he is issuing orders to get the campaign under way (Joshua 1:10–15).

If you've received a vision from God, you need to seize it too.

Don't waver or put it off. Stop trying to have all the answers before launching out in faith.

All God needs is all you've got. Give it to Him—today.

PRAYER FOCUS: Deal with God in prayer about what He's asking you to do today and about the things that are holding you back from it. Be bold. Commit to respond.

Sanctified Naiveté

*Brothers, think of what you were when you were
called. Not many of you were wise by human stan-
dards; not many were influential; not many were
of noble birth.*

—1 CORINTHIANS 1:26

Today's Bible reading: 1 Corinthians 1:18–31

After the initial detonation of my Page 23 vision, God kept con-
firming my passion to move to a major metropolitan area to start a
church. But here's the thing: I knew nothing about big cities. My
hometown had a population of six thousand people. We thought
a trip to Wal-Mart was an event to get all dressed up for. I knew
even less about starting a church. And I felt way too young to take
on such a serious task. But somehow I sensed none of this would
ultimately matter. When God speaks, He does not stutter.

I think I know why God gave me a bold vision for my life at
such a young age. He had to get to me before I was old enough to
know any better. See, audacious faith starts with sanctified naiveté.
And there's an unearned optimism that comes as standard equipment when you're young.

You might have your own sanctified naiveté. You could be in any season of life. You might be getting older and feeling as if you're running out of time. You might be young, as I was. You might be inexperienced. You might be poorly educated. You might be short on friends and funds, credentials and qualifications. From an objective standpoint, you might not look anything like heaven's pick for planting the impossible on the shores of the mundane.

If so, you're in great company.

The faith Jesus founded gained its popularity among nobodies. When we think about the congregations of the New Testament era, we have to think about the likes of everyday shopkeepers, day laborers, and stay-at-home moms. God planned it that way "so that no one may boast before him" (verse 29).

 RT Sometimes it's better if you don't know any better. #sunstandstill

---

But the undeniable fact is, these people went on to spread the underground revolution of grace in Jesus until it filtered into the whole known world. The greatest movement in the history of humanity sprang from the faith of audacious nobodies.

Maybe being naive and under-resourced isn't so bad after all.

Sometimes godly enthusiasm makes up for a lack of experience. Sometimes Spirit-filled determination compensates for a deficiency of knowledge. Sometimes sheer trust in God's vision trumps every reason why not. The legions of the naive can change reality just by being ready to walk into the visions God gives.

So don't despise your naiveté. If God is calling you to do something for Him today, take the first step.

Sometimes it's better if you don't know any better.

PRAYER FOCUS: Ask God to preserve your childlike faith in Him and to use your inadequacy to display His sufficiency.

Give Me My Rocks

Saul dressed David in his own tunic. He put a coat of
armor on him and a bronze helmet on his head. David
fastened on his sword over the tunic and tried walking
around, because he was not used to them.

"I cannot go in these," [David] said to Saul, "be-
cause I am not used to them."

—1 SAMUEL 17:38–39

Today's Bible reading: 1 Samuel 17:1–51

For days none of Israel's fighting men have been willing to con-
front the Philistine giant Goliath. Then David, a shepherd boy,
volunteers. King Saul instructs the equipment manager to bring
out the best armor and heaviest artillery Israel has to offer.

David tries it on, takes a test lap, and turns up his nose. "This
is nice," he says, "but it isn't for me. I have to work with what I
know. Somebody help me get out of this oversized armor and hand
me my sling."

In the end he wears what he always wears and uses the weapons he's familiar with—a leather sling and some smooth stones.

And the strategy pays off. (Audacity always does.) David kills the giant and saves the day.

In my early days as a pastor, a consultant suggested that the people of Charlotte weren't going to relate very well to my preaching style. I was confrontational and abrasive. They wanted conversational and inviting. If I really wanted to grow a church, he said, "Dial it down." Maybe I should "communicate" my "messages" sitting on a stool instead of running around. Above all else, I should keep it short. If I preached over thirty minutes, they wouldn't come back.

I tried that. It wasn't me.

Then one day I let loose. I didn't bother with a stool. I pretended like the clock in the back of the room wasn't there. I preached with authority and energy. With passion and edge. Loud and fast. And long. Some would say I shucked the corn that day. Whatever I did, it felt good. It felt authentic.

 RT God did not create you to fit in. He intends for you to stand out. #sunstandstill

---

For some reason the people came back in greater numbers the next week.

That's when a liberating realization flashed inside me: *God has been preparing me all my life for this. My anointing flows freely when I tap the vein of my unique abilities and my distinctive passion.*

Mediocrity is mass-produced. Destiny is custom designed.

Cookie-cutter Christianity dials down your distinctions. Audacity amplifies them.

You're never going to amount to half of what God has dreamed of you becoming unless you embrace the unique person God made you to be in the first place. He's made you on purpose for a purpose. You have a unique DNA with unique talents, passions, and experience that no one else on this earth has.

God did not create you to fit in. He intends for you to stand out.

PRAYER FOCUS: Ask God to help you understand better who He made you to be. Ask Him, too, for the courage to live out that identity with abandon as you go after the impossible dream He has given you.

God Is Bigger

As the heavens are higher than the earth,
so are my ways higher than your ways
and my thoughts than your thoughts.

—Isaiah 55:9

Today's Bible reading: Isaiah 55:6–13

Years ago I was preaching in a small town in South Carolina. The guy picked to drive me from the church to the house where I was staying was a Sunday school teacher. He was also a big, burly redneck.

In the car this guy started screaming at me about how unbiblical I'd been in the sermon I'd just preached at the church.

I had told a story in my sermon about how my dad had liver cancer and how we were praying that God would heal him. But even if my father wasn't healed, I'd said, we would still trust God.

My redneck driver began shouting at me, "I wouldn't want to have faith in a God who couldn't heal cancer. So if your dad doesn't recover from the cancer, we'll all know your family doesn't have enough faith."

We started arguing, and—honest to God—we almost got in a

fistfight when we reached my host's house. Some deacons from the church had to break it up.

The next day I sat down with the pastor and said, "I think you should know something about the chauffeur you appointed to run me back and forth." I explained how this man had said that if my dad wasn't healed, it would be because of my lack of faith.

 RT Faith is governed by laws and principles, but it can't be condensed into a magic formula. #sunstandstill

---

"He tells everybody that stuff," the pastor said. "One of the couples in his Sunday school class recently had a child who was stillborn. He used a Sunday morning session to teach them that they didn't have enough faith and that was the reason their child died." He added, "It caused a big commotion in the church."

You think?

You think having Dr. Dumbbell teach your Sunday school and propagate that junk is going to have a negative effect on people? It will do more than that. It will corrupt people's conception of the way God works. Do you need me to fire this clown for you?

Let's be clear about something: faith is governed by laws and principles, but it can't be condensed into a magic formula. God is way too big to be confined in some blab-it-and-grab-it formula of theology. His thoughts are not our thoughts, and His ways are not our ways.

"Seek the LORD while he may be found; call on him while he is near," Isaiah says (verse 6). *Of course* we should pray boldly for what we think is best. That's at the heart of the Sun Stand Still experience. But let's have enough humility to realize that sometimes God's will is not going to be what we expect, or when, or how.

What we have audacious faith for, ultimately, is God's plan, not our own.

PRAYER FOCUS: In prayer, ask God to help you align yourself with His plans and desires for your life.

The Perhaps Paradox

Come, let's go over to the outpost of those uncircumcised fellows. Perhaps the LORD will act in our behalf. Nothing can hinder the LORD from saving, whether by many or by few.

—1 SAMUEL 14:6

Today's Bible reading: 1 Samuel 14:1–14

In today's reading the army of King Saul has been locked in a standoff against the Philistines. And Jonathan, the king's son, has become so aggravated with the inaction of his fellow warriors that he decides to make a bold move. He enlists his armor bearer to join him on a two-man commando raid.

His battle plan is potentially God inspired—and a little ludicrous. The two young men will openly approach the enemy outpost. If they get a go-ahead sign from God, they will attack. A borderline suicide mission. But if God is with them, Jonathan figures, nothing can stop them.

In his motivational speech to his bodyguard, Jonathan seems to be speaking out of both sides of his mouth:

- Nothing can hinder the Lord.
- Perhaps the Lord will act.

At first glance this seems like spiritual schizophrenia.

But *perhaps* Jonathan isn't schizophrenic. *Perhaps* true faith always feels this way. On the one hand, I *know* that God is able to do anything. On the other hand, I *think* He's willing to do this specific thing. I know God can. And I'm pretty sure He will. But I can't be completely sure.

That's where audacious faith comes in.

Audacity isn't the absence of uncertainty and ambiguity. Audacity is believing that God's *promise* is bigger than my *perhaps.*

Sometimes I stand up in front of my church, share a logic-defying vision, and wrap it with a bodacious assertion: "I *know* I've heard from God about this." Maybe I should be more precise. When I say that, what I mean is "I'm as sure as I can be right now that I've heard from God about this."

 RT Audacity is believing that God's *promise* is bigger than my *perhaps.* #sunstandstill

---

The Bible says that God's Word is a lamp unto our feet (Psalm 119:105), not a floodlight beaming to our destination. So, armed with the confidence that there's a *decent chance* and an *interesting possibility* that my impulse *might* be from God (*perhaps,* in other words), I start investigating.

We'd all like to live in a world where God lets us do big things that require minimal risk. Where the voice of the Holy Spirit carries for miles and miles, piercing through static and fuzz, jeers and taunts. The fact is, though, that the land where the sun stands still is a land where *promise* and *perhaps* must coexist. Audacious faith does not eliminate doubt and fear. It eclipses their power one decision at a time. You know God's will by doing God's will.

Please don't wait until you have 100 percent certainty to follow Jesus boldly.

Jonathan and his armor bearer ended up saving the day in a spectacular way. Their act of audacious faith tilted the fate of an entire nation.

Act on your *perhaps,* and see what God will do in your world.

PRAYER FOCUS: Pray for growing clarity from God and for the guts to proceed even when you don't have all the answers.

Between the Promise and the Payoff

The seventh time the servant reported, "A cloud as small as a man's hand is rising from the sea."

—1 KINGS 18:44

Today's Bible reading: 1 Kings 18:41–46

Every big dream has a small beginning. No exceptions. Every tree was a seed once upon a time. The people who do big things for God are the ones who have the perspective to see the potential in these small beginnings. They refuse to stop nurturing the seed until the dream is full grown.

Consider Elijah. He assures King Ahab that a three-year drought is coming to an end. Then Elijah sends his servant to go and look toward the sea for signs of a rainstorm.

Nothing.

Six times the servant goes back to look. Six times nothing is there.

Then the seventh time a little bit of hope sticks out in the sky—a cloud as small as a man's hand.

Not long after that, the windows of heaven open, and the rain comes pouring down.

But before there is a downpour, there were three long years of parched ground, crop failure, and famine. And there was the faith of one man who held on to what he had heard, even when he couldn't see any signs in the sky.

The ability to stay tuned in to what you've heard from God when you can't see any proof that it's coming to pass is what separates audacious faith from wishful thinking.

One of my biggest Sun Stand Still prayers after I gave my life to Christ at age sixteen was that my dad would get into a right relationship with God. In the kitchen one evening, I said to him, "Dad, God is about to get hold of your life. And when He does, everything is going to change."

 RT Between the promise and the payoff, there's always a process. That process is where your audacious faith comes into play. #sunstandstill

---

He just nodded and kept on washing the dishes.

Three years later I preached at my home church. At the end of the sermon, I invited people to come to the altar and give their lives to Jesus. Soon I couldn't believe what I was seeing. My dad was kneeling at the altar, crying like a baby, dedicating his life to Christ.

Finally.

After twenty years of my mother praying and three years of my praying for my dad's salvation.

Embrace the reality that between the promise and the payoff, there's always a process. Without the process there is no progress. But the process is usually filled with pain. And if you don't know how to process the process, you probably won't make it to your promised land.

That's why audacious faith is so vital. It redirects your attention from what *is* right now to what you believe *will be* one day. And it ensures that you don't give up in the meantime—before you ever get to see your dream become a reality.

PRAYER FOCUS: If you're in the middle of a process, pray for God to help you stay faithful until you see signs that the payoff is near.

Mistake into Miracle

If we claim to be without sin, we deceive ourselves and the truth is not in us. If we confess our sins, he is faithful and just and will forgive us our sins and purify us from all unrighteousness.

—1 John 1:8–9

Today's Bible reading: 1 John 1:5–10

In *Sun Stand Still* I tell the story of Norm. He was one of the most beloved volunteers at our church. One afternoon Norm said to me, "Pastor, I think I'm going to prison soon."

Turns out that Norm had been involved in some illegal online activity before he accepted Christ. Now the law was catching up with him.

Norm pleaded guilty to all the charges. The judge sentenced him to serve forty-eight months in a federal prison.

Each of us has our personal catalog of screwups and failures. Maybe you did something stupid years ago and you're still paying for it. Maybe your mistakes are more recent. Maybe you haven't honored your marriage, haven't finished your degree, haven't paid your bills, haven't been there for your kids.

Maybe you're in real trouble right now, and you know in your heart that you have no one to blame but yourself.

Those are the hardest kinds of setbacks to overcome—the ones we create for ourselves. It's natural to see the potential for redemption when someone else fails. But when we fail, it can feel like the game is over.

Let me assure you that if you have a little bit of faith left, it's not over. Many people would say that God can still use you *in spite* of your failures. I want to take that a step further. God's grace is so audacious that He will use the *failure itself* to show off just how capable He is.

 RT God can't make anything miraculous out of your mistake if you don't call it what it is and deal with it accordingly. #sunstandstill

---

Nothing you've done is so repulsive that God can't redeem your potential and love you through it. But you have to face up to your wrongdoing before you can truly put it behind you.

Get honest about your failure. Assess the damage your sin has caused. Stop making excuses. Don't even try to play off the pain. Get it out in the open. If you've wronged someone, go to that person and seek forgiveness. If your sin is just between you and God, stop trying to hide it from Him, and spend some serious time confessing your sin to Him.

God can't make anything miraculous out of your mistake if you don't call it what it is and deal with it accordingly.

What I couldn't say when writing *Sun Stand Still* (because it hadn't happened yet) was that Norm has been released from jail after serving nearly all of his four-year sentence. When I first saw him after his release, I gave him a hug that maybe lasted longer than any hug I've given my wife or kids. I couldn't believe how great it felt to have him back.

That's how God feels about us when we repent and come back into His arms.

PRAYER FOCUS: If you have unconfessed sin in your life, ask for and receive God's forgiveness. Then move on in the direction He is calling you to.

Expect the Best

*"Lord, if it's you," Peter replied, "tell me to come to you
on the water."*

"Come," he said.

*Then Peter got down out of the boat, walked on
the water and came toward Jesus.*

—Matthew 14:28–29

Today's Bible reading: Matthew 14:22–31

I was having a conversation with someone, and at one point he
pulled out the classic saying "Expect the worst and hope for the
best." I know the heart behind this phrase. I know it means we
should prepare contingencies in case our plans fail. But still, I find
it to be a horrible saying.

The problem is that it misunderstands the nature of expectation. Expectation is a form of faith. Your expectation is the belief
that what you're hoping for is actually going to happen, not your
backup plan to take care of yourself in case it doesn't.

You can't hope for God's best if you're believing in the worst.
You can't hope to get the job you desperately need if you're expecting to get turned down. You can't hope that your kids are going to

become world changers if you're expecting them to be juvenile delinquents. You can't hope that God is going to restore your marriage if you're expecting to sign divorce papers any day now.

What would Peter have done that day out on the Sea of Galilee if he had expected the worst and hoped for the best? Well, his name means "Rock," and I suppose he would have expected to sink like one. This terrible expectation would have been offset at best by a hope that Jesus would grab his arm and pull him back to the surface before he drowned.

But that's not what is going through Peter's mind. Peter—at least at first—expects the best. Since Jesus calls him out of the boat, well, then Peter apparently thinks he will be able to go to Him walking on the waves.

 RT You can't hope for the best if you're believing in the worst. #sunstandstill

---

Now, it's true that in just a moment his fear will get the better of him. His faith will cease holding him up, and he will earn a rebuke from the Lord because of it. But let's give him his props. At least for a little while, he really believes he can walk on water—and he does it.

How many of us have such a strong expectation of the best that we are prepared to lower ourselves over the side of the boat and place the ball of our foot onto the uncertainty of water?

Jesus is calling you today. "Come to Me," He says. "Come toward the future I have for you."

And so expect the best. Hope for the best. Accept what God allows. And give Him the glory.

PRAYER FOCUS: Seek God's help to expect the best in fulfilling the vision He has given you.

Spontaneous Obedience

As they traveled along the road, they came to some
water and the eunuch said, "Look, here is water. Why
shouldn't I be baptized?"

—Acts 8:36

Today's Bible reading: Acts 8:26–39

Have you ever noticed that some of the biggest opportunities in life come at a time and in a way you don't expect? And not only that, but also the response we need to make to those opportunities is often just a simple step.

Holly can tell you this about the day I asked her to marry me. She had no idea it was coming, but it was the single greatest event of her entire existence. (I'm kidding, you know...or am I?) That's why they call it popping the question, because you have to pop it. You know, sneak up behind her and—*pow!*—give her the rock. Put a ring on it.

One Sunday I surprised the people who showed up at our church. I said, "We've been planning on doing baptisms this week-end for a long time, but what you may not have known is that there's a good chance *you're* going to be one of the people getting baptized." *Pow!*

Then I preached my heart out about Philip and the Ethiopian eunuch in Acts 8.

Philip uses the Scriptures to put together the pieces about Jesus for the Ethiopian, apparently including baptism as a sign of following Him. And it turns out the Ethiopian is a let's-get-this-started kind of guy.

"Look, here is water," the Ethiopian says to Philip. "Why shouldn't I be baptized?"

Why not?

The fact is, there is no reason why he shouldn't be baptized then and there. So the chariot comes to a screeching halt, and inside of a minute he and Philip are down in the water, completing the act of obedience.

 RT Some of the greatest moments of your life will come when you least expect it, through a simple step. #sunstandstill

---

And this, I explained to my congregation, was why many of them were going to get baptized.

Hurrying on, I didn't leave them with one excuse to put off getting baptized that very day.

You say you have nothing to wear in the water? We provided T-shirts, shorts, and flip-flops—blue for the guys and pink for the girls. We even had unmentionables for them so they didn't have to go home wet.

Worried about what your hair will look like afterward? We had hairbrushes, hair products, and blow dryers on hand.

We had security guards standing by to protect their belongings while they were getting baptized.

We had professional photographers waiting in the wings to record the moment so they could share the event with their loved ones who weren't present.

The dam broke. We baptized hundreds of people that day.

What do you feel God is calling you to do today? Ask yourself, *Why not?* The sooner you step into the water, the sooner you can go on your way rejoicing.

PRAYER FOCUS: Spend time with God asking Him what you can do to follow Him faithfully, not tomorrow, not the day after tomorrow, but today.

Whose Idea
Was That?

I tell you the truth, if you have faith and do not doubt...
you can say to this mountain, "Go, throw yourself into
the sea," and it will be done.

—MATTHEW 21:21

Today's Bible reading: Matthew 21:18–22

When you look at the miracles in the Bible, you see two themes
emerge:

1. Many biblical miracles were the person's own initiative,
   not God's idea.
2. Many biblical miracles involved the person's own natural
   action, not just God's supernatural intervention.

Don't believe me? Let's look at some examples.

First, *whose initiative?*

When Jesus healed a woman who had been bleeding for twelve
years, who initiated that event? The woman herself touched the
hem of Jesus's garment, drawing out Jesus's power (Luke 8:43–48).

When the Syrian general Naaman was healed of leprosy, how

did that get started? Naaman acted on a tip and sought out the prophet Elisha for healing (2 Kings 5:1–19).

Now, second, *whose action*? Consider…

The blind man in Jerusalem didn't get his sight back immediately when Jesus pressed a mud pie to his eyes. Jesus told him to go and wash in the pool of Siloam (John 9:1–7).

The walls of Jericho didn't fall simply because of a word from the Lord. Before that, Joshua and his army marched around the city for seven days and blew trumpets (Joshua 6:1–20).

The bottom line for you is that, when it comes to the miracles you want to see in and through your life, God wants your involvement.

 RT Without God, you cannot. Without you, God will not. #sunstandstill

---

But are you ready for it?

Maybe this isn't true for you, but the sad fact is that most Christians don't want miracles; we want magic. We want God to wave a wand at our problem or our need and instantly clear it up—without our taking any responsibility whatsoever.

We're in debt, and we want God to send us money out of the sky. God forbid that we should cut up our credit cards!

We're in a pattern of poor health and want God to heal us of our physical ailments. We would never think of changing our eating habits and starting an exercise regimen.

We're stuck in the ordinary and want to see God do miraculous things through us. Who would think that we would develop some skills to give God a platform from which He can operate in our lives?

Of course God's miracles involve His unmistakable power and provision—otherwise they wouldn't be miracles. But they also require our initiative and involvement. Maybe we could sum it up like this: Without God, you cannot. Without you, God will not.

PRAYER FOCUS: What involvement is God requiring from you before He accomplishes a miracle in your life? Pray about what you should do.

Hear the Word

Faith comes from hearing the message, and the message is heard through the word of Christ.

—ROMANS 10:17

Today's Bible reading: Romans 10:14–21

There's only one place you can acquire audacious faith, the kind of faith that dares to believe God for the impossible. You have to go to the Bible—the Word of God.

Faith development goes through a process, and it looks like this:

- Hearing the Word of God initiates your faith.
- Speaking the Word of God activates your faith.
- Doing the Word of God demonstrates your faith.

We'll get to *speaking* and *doing* the Word of God and the benefits they bring in the next couple of days. But it all starts with *hearing*.

More than once I've told my congregation something like this: "At Elevation Church we try to surprise you with something new every time you show up. But there is one surprise I'll never pull on you. I'll never walk up on stage without my Bible in my hand to teach you the Word of God." When it comes down to it, the Word of God is the only thing I can bring them that's going to be transformative, that's going to change their world.

In the same way, as you are using the *Sun Stand Still Devotional,* I hope you aren't just reading my words on the page. I hope you're reading the daily Bible passage and using it as a springboard for prayer. I hope you're reading each passage slowly. Pondering it to get everything you can out of it. Opening your heart to let it come in and search you and change you.

 RT The only way you're going to get audacious faith is to hear God's Word and consume it. #sunstandstill

---

In fact, you're wise to take advantage of *any* sound tool that helps you encounter God's Word and the Savior at the center of it. Sermons. Christian books. Bible commentaries. Sunday school classes. Bible-study groups or courses. Podcasts. Reading plans on YouVersion. Or whatever you can get your hands on. These things are an investment in your faith formation.

The simple fact is, the only way you're going to get audacious faith is to hear God's Word and consume it. After all, you can't claim God's promises if you don't know God's promises. So you have to saturate your mind with the Scriptures.

In his letter to the Romans, the apostle Paul writes that we are saved when we call on the name of the Lord. That's Step 5, as he outlines it. He walks the process backward in Romans 10:14–15.

Step 4: "How, then, can they call on the one they have not believed in?"

Step 3: "And how can they believe in the one of whom they have not heard?"

Step 2: "And how can they hear without someone preaching to them?"

Step 1: "And how can they preach unless they are sent?"

Check out Step 3 again. At the center of the process is hearing.

When you hear the Word, it initiates your faith. "Faith comes from hearing the message" (verse 17).

Want more faith? Put yourself in the way of the Word.

PRAYER FOCUS: Pick phrases out of Psalm 119 to help you tell God how much you love His Word and want to know it intimately.

Speak the Word

Do not let this Book of the Law depart from your
mouth; meditate on it day and night, so that you
may be careful to do everything written in it.

—JOSHUA 1:8

Today's Bible reading: Joshua 1:6–9

When Joshua is starting out his career as top leader of the Hebrew
nation, God gives him the command recorded in Joshua 1:8. Now,
I think most of us subconsciously translate that command to
mean: Do not let this book of the Law depart from your *heart.* Or
from your *mind.* But that's not what God says. He specifically tells
Joshua to keep His Word in his *mouth.* Before Joshua can make the
sun stand still, he has to make the ways and words of God a natural
part of his vocabulary—in speaking to others and in speaking to
himself.

Every time before I preach, I go through a kind of pregame
ritual. I take a bottle of oil and anoint different parts of my body—
my hands, my feet, my belly, my heart, my mouth, my eyes, my
ears, my head. And as I anoint each part, I speak an appropriate
verse of Scripture. By the time I've gone through that whole pro-

cess, God's Word has come forth from my mouth, my faith is acti-
vated, and I'm ready to deliver the message God has given me.

This little ritual may sound superstitious, but it's so important
to me to be in the right place spiritually every single time I open
my mouth to preach on behalf of Jesus.

Let me assure you: this speaking-the-Word thing isn't just for
preachers like me and Bible heroes like Joshua. If you want to get
really good at walking in audacious faith, you have to get really
good at preaching God's Word to yourself.

 RT Quit telling God how big your mountain is and
start telling your mountain how big your God is.
#sunstandstill

See, there are going to be many points along the way when
you won't have anyone around to motivate you or encourage you.
And in those moments you'd better be able to open God's Word,
look in the mirror, and remind yourself of the truth. As you incor-
porate God's Word into your vocabulary, the way you see your
circumstances will begin to shift. Your faith will start to rise higher
than your feelings and your fears. This all comes through speaking
the Word.

Just imagine how much difference it would make in your life
if you would preach God's Word to yourself. As I heard an elderly
preacher say, quit telling God how big your mountain is and start
telling your mountain how big your God is.

Preach God's Word to yourself. Daily and passionately. Maybe you don't feel qualified. Well, by the authority of Christ vested in me, I hereby ordain you as a minister of the gospel to preach to yourself. (I wouldn't advise you to perform any weddings or funerals, as they will not be recognized legally.)

PRAYER FOCUS: Ask God to lead you to scriptures that relate to the struggles and pressures of your life so that you can begin to preach to yourself.

Do the Word

We are God's workmanship, created in Christ Jesus to do good works, which God prepared in advance for us to do.

—Ephesians 2:10

Today's Bible reading: Ephesians 2:1–10

It's possible for us to hear God's Word, take notes, memorize Scripture, and speak God's Word out loud until everybody thinks we're smoking something yet never walk in true, audacious faith. Because it's not really faith until we do it. Authentic faith doesn't end in a positive mental state. It plays out in total obedience based on the sure Word of God. That's how we demonstrate our faith.

We Christians like to talk about how grace comes through faith and not by works. All true and wonderful. But let's not take it to an extreme where we start to think that obedience to God's Word (the Bible) or God's word to us (such as our Page 23 vision) is somehow irrelevant or unimportant. The very passage in the Bible that talks about grace coming through faith also states that God's purpose for us is that we will "*do* good works, which God prepared in advance for us *to do*" (verses 8–10). There it is: do.

Let's be clear: there isn't some kind of minimum obedience level you must reach in order to qualify for a miracle from God. Audacious faith is possible and intended for every believer in Jesus. In fact, as I said earlier, God often uses our failures for His glory in stunning ways—mistakes into miracles. But still, we're at our best when we have a hunger for righteousness burning inside and a heart that aches every time we grieve the Holy Spirit with our sin.

 RT Authentic faith doesn't end in a positive mental state. It plays out in total obedience based on the sure Word of God. #sunstandstill

---

Doing the Word by obeying God's commands is the capstone of the faith-formation process for every audacious Christian. We have to care about obedience.

When Elevation grew from just a few families to over a thousand people, I started realizing how the devil had a bull's-eye on my soul. Many pastors develop secret lives of habitual sin. Then they wind up melting down in the spotlight for the world to see, hurting a lot of people and damaging the testimony of Jesus. By God's grace I wasn't there yet or anywhere close. But with the stress and pace of ministry, I was afraid I could be one day.

So I started seeing a professional Christian counselor. He helped me avoid sin and stay pure so that nothing would hinder God's vision for my life. That's one way I have chosen to prioritize and pursue obedience to God.

The link between faith and fruitfulness for God is doing the Word. Don't let carelessness about holiness rob you of your miracle.

PRAYER FOCUS: Ask God to show you where you need to seek His forgiveness for sin, reform your habits, or put in place guardrails for your moral life.

March All Night

*Faith by itself, if it is not accompanied by
action, is dead.*

—James 2:17

Today's Bible reading: James 2:14–26

For seventeen days I have been encouraging you to have audacious faith and pray Sun Stand Still prayers. But now I want to point out something else big from the story of Joshua at the battle of Gibeon. Yes, Joshua had the faith to pray an audacious prayer. And, yes, God stopped the sun in the middle of the sky as a result.

But Joshua had to fight the battle for himself.

Asking and acting go hand in hand. And sometimes the action that faith requires is quite demanding.

Joshua 10:9 casually slips in "After an all-night march from Gilgal..."

An all-night march? Lugging weapons and supplies through enemy territory in the dark? Twenty miles *uphill* only hours before the biggest battle of the campaign?

This puts faith in a different perspective.

Joshua's big prayer wasn't a cop-out. He didn't ask God to make the sun stand still while kneeling in the comfort of his tent. He did it on his feet after an all-night march and an all-day battle.

Sometimes when we need a miracle from God, we have a tendency to divorce His part from our part. Isn't that right? We say things like "Well, all we can do now is pray."

That's shortsighted on multiple levels.

 RT Asking and acting go hand in hand.
#sunstandstill

For one thing, why are we talking about prayer like it's the last kid picked for dodge ball? Prayer is not our last resort; it's our highest appeal. Joshua said everything he needed to say to God in one sentence, and it led to the sun standing still in the sky. So prayer isn't anemic (though our approach to it might be).

Furthermore, "All we can do now is pray" ignores the fact that we can be asking *and* acting, doing *and* praying. Joshua prayed his prayer, then he got back to fighting. Although God threw down hailstones, the Israelite army had to use their swords too. The sun stood still, not so that the soldiers could take a break, but so that they could keep on doing their job.

The apostle James tries to remarry what we have divorced. Faith doesn't even exist, he says, without deeds. He even constructs a hypothetical argument to prove the absurdity of this approach. James throws out there, "Someone will say, 'You have faith; I have deeds' " (James 2:18). As if we can specialize in either believing or doing, then leave the other virtue up to someone else.

James laughs in the face of this faulty logic. "Show me your faith without deeds, and I will show you my faith by what I do" (verse 18). If you think you can have audacious belief without good works to match, you really have neither one. The proof of faith is the action it produces.

What work should you be doing today to demonstrate your faith?

What God has joined, let no one separate.

PRAYER FOCUS: Ask God's forgiveness if you have been slacking on the work He's calling you to do.

The Surcharge of Sacrifice

The Lord said to Joshua, "Make flint knives and circumcise the Israelites again." So Joshua made flint knives and circumcised the Israelites at Gibeath Haaraloth.

—Joshua 5:2–3

Today's Bible reading: Joshua 5:1–9

A high calling for your life is God's gift to you. It's not something you earn. But you don't get to participate in a high calling without paying a high cost.

You will, in fact, pay a tremendous price to operate in a great anointing. And the level of your impact will be directly proportionate to the price you are willing to pay. Here's one way to look at it: Faith is included in the contract of salvation. But activating your faith to realize God's vision for your life involves a surcharge of sacrifice.

Just before Joshua marches around Jericho, an event happens that I don't remember hearing about in Sunday school. God tells

Joshua to make flint knives and circumcise all the Israelite men. And Joshua does it.

Ouch.

To the Hebrew people, male circumcision was a physical sign of a spiritual covenant between the people and God. It was an extremely meaningful event, signifying God's promise to His people as well as their commitment to His commands.

In the New Testament the ritual takes on a different meaning. The apostle Paul talks about a "circumcision of the heart," one that isn't "merely outward and physical" (Romans 2:28–29). This circumcision involves God's cutting away everything in our lives that doesn't bring glory to Him. Stripping away our pride and self-reliance. Teaching us to trust only in Him.

 RT You don't get to participate in a high calling without paying a high cost. #sunstandstill

---

If we're going to live lives based on believing God for the impossible, our hearts will have to be circumcised. We'll have to go under the knife. We'll have to choose to take some costly steps of obedience to really follow Christ in audacious faith.

I don't know exactly what the cutting-away process will look like for you, but remember this: when God cuts something out of your life, it's because He wants to bring something better. Sometimes God has to let your dream die so that His vision for you can come alive. I've met many great men and women of God who pinpoint the most confusing and agonizing failures of their lives as the impetus for their most significant spiritual advancement.

If God comes toward you with the flint knife today, remember that He's not out to hurt you. He's aligning your desires with His so that He can accomplish the impossible in your life. And once you've made up your mind to pay the price and to trust the Lord with all your heart, no level of spiritual achievement will be out of reach. Because when you want what God wants for the reasons He wants it, you're unstoppable.

A high calling often exacts a high price. But it always yields a supernatural return.

PRAYER FOCUS: Ask God to show you what He wants to cut away from your life so you will be better suited to serve Him—and to help you cooperate with the operation, painful though it may be.

Building on Hope

Faith is the substance of things hoped for,
the evidence of things not seen.

—HEBREWS 11:1, KJV

Today's Bible reading: Hebrews 11:1–16

A lot of people confuse faith and hope. They think they're walking in faith when actually all they're doing is standing in hope.

If we want to have audacious faith—faith that dares to believe God for the impossible—then we need to make sure we're distinguishing it from hope. Not that there's anything wrong with hope. Hope is crucial. But the Scriptures make it clear that, although the two work hand in hand, faith and hope perform different functions.

It has really helped me to look at it this way: hope is the blueprint; faith is the contractor. That's what the writer of Hebrews is getting at: "Faith is the *substance* of things hoped for." So when I hope for something, my faith is the connection between my hope and the manifestation of that which I'm hoping for.

Most of my life I imagined faith as some kind of force field.

And the way we talk about faith dematerializes it. By most definitions faith is synonymous with hope.

The more I study Scripture, though, the more I detect this distinction: Hope is a *desire*. Faith is a *demonstration*. Hope *wants* it to happen. Faith *causes* it to happen and acts as if it's already done.

Faith is not an abstract theoretical proposition. It's not wishful thinking. It's substance. It's action.

It's good to hope for things. It's good to hope for financial provision so that you can take care of yourself and your family. It's good to hope for someone to love and to share your life with. It's good to hope for improved health when you're sick.

 RT Hope is the blueprint; faith is the contractor.
#sunstandstill

But remember, hope is not faith. Faith is the contractor. Like hope, it operates before the fulfillment, but it's active in trying to help bring that fulfillment about.

Let's say you and your spouse hope to have a child. The doctors have been telling you that you're not going to have a child. So what do you do next? I've had people in this situation tell me, "But we're praying for a baby." Great. But that's not all you can do. Faith not only prays; it also pursues.

Do all that you can to have a baby. Have fun while you're at it.

If you need to see specialists, save up your money and go to the specialists.

If you finally come to believe that God is saying you'll never have a baby of your own, maybe you should look into adopting a baby, either domestically or internationally.

And if God doesn't seem to be leading you in those directions, maybe He has something else in mind. Maybe you'll be like my friends who, although they have no natural children, have been richly blessed with spiritual children all over the world, whom they have discipled through two decades of faithful and fruitful ministry.

There are so many steps of faith you can take to participate with God in the fulfillment of your hope.

Obviously, hoping for a baby is just one example. But whatever you're hoping for today, remember to take one step at a time, walking in faith. Do all you can do and keep trusting God to do what only He can do. That's real faith. It consults God's blueprint and gets to work building the reality, for His glory.

PRAYER FOCUS: Ask God to help you see how to use your faith to build substance out of your godly hopes and desires.

Faith Forensics

Some faced jeers and flogging, while still others were
chained and put in prison. They were stoned; they
were sawed in two; they were put to death by the
sword.... The world was not worthy of them.

—Hebrews 11:36–38

Today's Bible reading: Hebrews 11:17–40

How has your faith been developing in recent days, months, or
years? Maybe it hasn't been developing so much as decreasing.

Maybe you feel like you're running out of time and the sun is
sinking low. Maybe you've adjusted your expectations to believe
that God is no bigger than the accomplishments of your human
effort. But I believe God wants to raise the stakes on your faith.

So many Christians live in a state of chronic and perpetual
discouragement. Things don't seem to be going well, and we don't
expect anything miraculous from God. So we hold on to our faith
like a Snuggie. Or we swallow it like an Ambien just to help us get
some sleep.

Sun Stand Still faith isn't like that. Sun Stand Still faith looks
at a situation that seems hopeless and finds hope. I don't care what

you're dealing with today. It's not more difficult than what Joshua faced. And it was child's play for God to stop the sun over Gibeon. There's always hope.

Faith is not a drug to sedate you through a life you hate. It's not a magic pill to make all your problems go away. It's a force to transport you to another realm of reality.

A lot of people use faith as a coping mechanism. Faith is not a coping mechanism; it is your weapon of mass destruction to win your spiritual war. The purpose of faith is to change your situation for the glory of God.

 RT Faith is not a drug to sedate you through a life you hate. It's a force to transport you to another realm of reality. #sunstandstill

---

So, on the one hand, you have some people who think faith means nothing bad will ever happen to you. Apparently they've never read to the end of Hebrews 11, where the Bible talks about people who were sawn in half for their faith. *Because* of their faith, not *in spite of* their faith. Not because they didn't have enough faith.

What good would faith be if you never needed it in the darkest valleys of your life? After all, the One we model our faith on went to a cross because of His faith in His Father.

On the other extreme, there are people who hold on to faith like a paci and a blanket. Like, "I don't have a job, but I have my faith."

Chances are, God is calling you, not only to have faith that He can give you a job, but also to have faith enough to put together a résumé, put some product in your hair, bring your best in a job interview, and find a way to feed your family. We have to resist the proclivity to skip the practical part and blame our lack of results on God.

Faith is supernatural. But it operates in the real world of struggle and striving.

PRAYER FOCUS: Pray for God to reveal to you today how you may have been thinking of faith in a way that's counterproductive to what He wants to do in your life.

What Are You More Afraid Of?

Another servant came and said, "Sir, here is your
mina; I have kept it laid away in a piece of cloth.
I was afraid of you, because you are a hard man."

—LUKE 19:20–21

Today's Bible reading: Luke 19:11–27

What are you more afraid of? The high cost of failure or the higher cost of missed opportunity? The pain of messing up or the deeper pain of missing out? Making the wrong decision or deciding by not deciding at all? Falling down or standing still?

The staff at our church has had to answer these soul-searching questions as we've sought to have a Sun Stand Still faith for our church and our city. We've decided that often it's better to regret something we did than something we didn't do. And I think this is the way all of us ought to live if we want to have audacious faith.

I know there are exceptions. Obviously, I'm not encouraging anybody to try their hand at sin and crime. Don't overanalyze this. Flow with me.

You have to decide. In your own life what are you more afraid of? Risking it all or wasting your life?

We need to know what fear means for us.

In one of His more startling pronouncements, Jesus says, "I tell you, my friends, do not be afraid of those who kill the body and after that can do no more. But I will show you whom you should fear: Fear him who, after the killing of the body, has power to throw you into hell. Yes, I tell you, fear him" (Luke 12:4–5).

Who is the one who "has power to throw you into hell"? Well, that's God.

 RT Often it's better to regret something you did than something you didn't do. #sunstandstill

---

Not that Jesus wants you cringing before God all the time. Jesus's sacrifice on the cross made it possible for us to receive the love and acceptance of God. But still, there's such a thing as healthy respect for God, isn't there? A part of that healthy respect is wanting His approval—not the world's approval—for what we do. And playing it safe rarely earns God's approval.

An *un*healthy fear of God shows up in Jesus's parable of the minas. This is another startling teaching by Jesus. The third servant in the parable gives in to his fear and decides to hide the assets his master gave him to invest. Everything's all right while the master's away. But when the master comes for an accounting, he angrily demands, "Couldn't you have done *something* with it?"

Serving God will cost you something. But there's also such a thing as opportunity cost—what you miss out on if you fail to act. Don't let your fears, worries, and self-doubts prevent you from acting on the vision God has given you. The cost of faith is great, but the cost of unbelief is much greater.

PRAYER FOCUS: Commit before God today to take hold of whatever opportunity He places before you, even if it seems risky.

Wave Jumper

The Lord will fight for you; you need only to be still.

—Exodus 14:14

Today's Bible reading: Exodus 14:5–31

When my son Elijah was smaller, he and I used to have a great time playing Wave Jumper at the beach.

We'd wade out into the ocean. The whole time I'd stand behind Elijah, holding his hands above his head. Every time a wave would arrive, just before the water would wipe him out, I'd jerk him up and keep him safe from the wave. Elijah would laugh uncontrollably and proudly announce, "I'm the Wave Jumper!"

I didn't (and still don't) have the heart to explain to my boy that, technically, he never was really much of a Wave Jumper. Daddy was doing all the heavy lifting. He should probably have been screaming something like "I'm the Hand Holder!"

It's a pretty silly, basic illustration, but it demonstrates one of the most common patterns in Scripture: as the big waves roll toward us, God promises to do the heavy lifting. He only requires that we have the faith to wade in as deep as He leads and to keep reaching up to Him.

When the people of Israel finally escape Egyptian slavery, God leads them through the desert toward an impassable barrier—the Red Sea. And there, with Pharaoh's army closing in, they are trapped. What can God's people do? If they stay on the shore, they'll be murdered. If they walk into the depths, they'll surely drown. No wonder the Bible says they mill around in confusion, crying out in terror.

 RT If you'll do the believing, God will do the achieving. #sunstandstill

---

Then Moses announces what will happen next: The Lord will fight for them. They only need to be still.

Translation: it may be your job to cross over, but it's God's job to see you through.

If you'll do the believing, God will do the achieving.

And before the Hebrews' eyes, He parts the waters so they can cross over in safety. (The Egyptian soldiers aren't so lucky.)

I hate to break this to you, because it might deflate your self-esteem. But technically, you're not much of a Wave Jumper. Yes, the risks of walking in faith are real. No, it's not a game. But remember, you're not alone in this by a long shot. Not only are you not alone, but you're not even primarily responsible for the outcome of your obedience. Your heavenly Father has a firm grip on you. His vantage point is way above the water level. He's bigger than you. He's stronger than you. And He's got you.

It gets even better: When you get down to it, you're not the one holding on to Him. He's holding on to you. Maybe you're afraid that if you pray a Sun Stand Still prayer and live by audacious faith, you'll end up letting God down. But the reality is, you were never holding Him up.

Whatever wave you face today, remember: You might not be much of a jumper. But you're safe in the hands of the One who stands above the wind and the waves.

PRAYER FOCUS: Thank your heavenly Father for how He protects, preserves, and sustains you through everything.

Up to Here in Fear

*Peace I leave with you; my peace I give you. I do not
give to you as the world gives. Do not let your hearts
be troubled and do not be afraid.*

—JOHN 14:27

Today's Bible reading: John 14:1–31

Anywhere there's great faith, there will also be equal and opposite
fear. So when you reflect on God's vision for your life, it's natural
if you feel overwhelmed. I know I did when I was starting a new
church in a big city.

It's not wrong to feel fear. It is wrong to let that fear have the
last word in your life.

The people who accomplish the most astounding things for
God's glory aren't the people who feel the least fear. Often they're
the ones who deal with the most intense amounts of fear. But instead of letting that fear disable their dreams, they start increasing
their capacity for faith. They act on the part of God's direction they
do understand. And they leave the rest up to Him.

When the synagogue ruler Jairus hears a report that his daughter has died, he naturally feels fear. But Jesus says something amazing to him: "Don't be afraid; just believe" (Mark 5:36).

On the surface that seems cold and callous. And it is...unless Jesus knows something Jairus doesn't know. Unless He is planning to do something for Jairus that Jairus can't do for himself.

In fact, He is. Jesus raises the dead daughter to life.

Jesus's attitude has not changed by the time He's facing the reality of His own death. He's intent on comforting His disciples, who are going to be separated from Him. And yet, really, they will not be separated. Because His death will not be the end of Him. And because the Holy Spirit will be a connecting line between these men and their Savior while they're physically apart. So His words to them are "Peace" and "Do not be afraid."

 RT Fear is like a telemarketer. The best strategy is to never even pick up the phone. #sunstandstill

---

What we see as a permanent condition, Jesus sees as a temporary circumstance. What we see as the end of the story, God sees as the beginning of our most miraculous chapter. He has resurrection power in His back pocket. He has something coming only He knows about.

Don't be afraid; just believe. God is planning to act on your behalf.

Here's what it comes to: Fear is like a telemarketer. The best strategy is to never even pick up the phone. Ignore it.

Just believe.

Do not let your heart be troubled, no matter how hard it tries to be.

PRAYER FOCUS: Ask God's help to defeat your fear with your faith.

DAY 25

Connector to
the Current

*It was [Christ] who gave some to be apostles, some to
be prophets, some to be evangelists, and some to be
pastors and teachers, to prepare God's people for works
of service.*

—Ephesians 4:11–12

Today's Bible reading: Ephesians 4:1–16

Certain phrases should be permanently banned from our Christian vocabulary. The one that sets me off the most is *full-time ministry.* I know what it's supposed to mean, but I vehemently disagree with its implications. To say that someone is called to full-time ministry suggests that others are permitted to do part-time ministry. There's no such thing as a part-time Christian, and there's no such thing as part-time ministry.

A very small percentage of Christians derive their livelihood from a religious institution. So you may work in the educational, legal, medical, financial, or some other industry. But no matter who pays your salary, you're a full-time employee of the kingdom of God. And wherever you work, that's your ministry. Whatever you're good at, that's your calling. In this way every component of your assignment has deep significance.

Every business negotiation you engage in is an opportunity for Christ to shine through you. Every teachable moment with your children is a bright spot in the making. Everywhere you set your foot is potential holy ground.

I teach our people at Elevation that the day I became their pastor, I left the ministry. I'm pretty sure Rick Warren said this before me, and I'm completely sure the apostle Paul said it before him. Ephesians 4:11–12 explains that the only job pastors and teachers have is to prepare God's people for their own personal ministry. So if the people don't have a ministry, I don't have a job.

 RT God conceals His extraordinary intentions in ordinary people to protect the extraordinary value of His purpose in our lives. #sunstandstill

---

I want the people in our church to see themselves as marketplace missionaries. Their profession is their pulpit. They are the image of God within the sphere of their influence. They are connectors to the current of the power of Christ; the grace of Christ flows through them into the lives of those they serve.

Sometimes audacity shimmers and shines. Most of the time the packaging is nondescript. I like to think God conceals His extraordinary intentions in ordinary people to protect the extraordinary value of His purpose in our lives.

When Jesus opened for business, He enlisted ordinary people skilled in ordinary ways. Wouldn't a rabbinical school have provided a more appropriate disciple-candidate pool than a family fishing business? There was no shortage of talent in the seminaries of Jesus's day, but He passed over the MDivs and scooped up a collection agent named Matthew.

And Jesus's affinity for the ordinary didn't stop with His selection process. Over the course of His three-year earthly ministry, most of His recorded miracles happened in the marketplace or by the side of the road, not in the synagogue. Put that in your theological pipe and take a toke.

Your Sun Stand Still assignment might not be meteoric. It might be mundane. But when you give all you've got for the cause of the One who gave it all to you in the first place, the effects of your investment will literally reach the heavens.

PRAYER FOCUS: Ask God to help you see the opportunities to represent Him in your everyday life.

Confident Humility

Lord, I do not deserve to have you come under my roof.
But just say the word, and my servant will be healed.

—MATTHEW 8:8

Today's Bible reading: Matthew 8:5–13

Praying audacious prayers and walking in bold faith obviously take confidence. But healthy confidence is born out of genuine humility. The two must work in tandem. Confidence without humility is arrogance. Humility without confidence is timidity. Confidence and humility are both biblical. And they're equally essential for a life of true faith.

One day a leading military official approaches Jesus. One of his most valuable servants is sick, and the outcome looks bleak. Jesus offers to abort His scheduled ministry activities and make a house call to heal the servant, but the commander suggests an alternative. Study his response in Matthew 8:8. It's a textbook lesson in audacious faith bolstered by confident humility:

- "Lord, I do not deserve to have you come under my roof." Humility.

- "But just say the word, and my servant will be healed."
  Confidence.

Complete confidence in the competency of Christ matched with sincere humility about oneself. This is the only formula for authentic audacious faith.

Apathy refuses to take the chance. Arrogance places you outside God's protective parameters. Either way, you'll miss out on the action if you aren't willing to get in over your head.

 RT Confidence without humility is arrogance. Humility without confidence is timidity. #sunstandstill

---

I would have been much more comfortable spending my life in a smaller town, like the one I grew up in. That wouldn't have been wrong, and for many people it would be exactly what God has called them to do. But in my Page 23 vision, God specifically called me to a big city for ministry. So I swallowed hard, took a deep breath, and decided to obey. It was *God* calling, after all. He had a plan, and I realized that the safest place for me was right in the middle of it.

When I step out on stage at Elevation or accept an invitation to speak at an event somewhere around the world, I still have moments when I start to doubt myself. Why me? But I remind myself, it really isn't about me. God is working His plan through me. And it could as easily be somebody else. But in this moment, for this purpose, God has chosen *me*.

Don't be like so many Christians who never wade into deep waters for fear of stingrays, sharks, and undertows. The One who creates, commands, and calms the waves is also able to keep you from going under.

At the same time, don't get overconfident in your own abilities to do something great for God. You'll end up thrashing around in self-reliance rather than clinging to God in faith. You have to be careful. Otherwise you'll mistake arrogance for audacity. As Jesus taught, "You also, when you have done everything you were told to do, should say, 'We are unworthy servants; we have only done our duty' " (Luke 17:10).

PRAYER FOCUS: Invite God to show you today how you may have been erring on the side of having too much confidence in yourself or on the side of having too little confidence in Him.

Pray like a Juggernaut

This is the confidence we have in approaching God:
that if we ask anything according to his will, he hears
us. And if we know that he hears us—whatever we
ask—we know that we have what we asked of him.

—1 John 5:14–15

Today's Bible reading: 1 John 5:1–15

Has your prayer life been changing as you've been working your way through the *Sun Stand Still Devotional*? I hope you're beginning to pray with more boldness and more faith, even if your progress seems small and subtle so far.

What I've observed is that, when it comes to prayer, a lot of us have the standard stuff down. But praying a Sun Stand Still prayer requires something more than general competence. It isn't like asking God to give you a good parking place on Black Friday or bless your pepperoni pizza "to the nourishment" of your body. It's wrapped with urgency. It's filled with possibility. And for most of us, it's a whole new way to pray.

I call it praying like a juggernaut. A juggernaut is defined as a large, overpowering, crushing force in motion.

First John 5:14–15 is a classic juggernaut prayer passage. It says that if we ask anything according to God's will, He will hear us and give us what we ask.

Notice that it doesn't say "if we ask anything we desire" or "if we ask anything audaciously," but "if we ask anything *according to his will*." In other words God wants our agenda to align with His will. Our audacity must be in sync with God's purposes.

Praying this way reconciles your dreams with the God you actually find in the Bible. At the same time it infinitely expands the scope of your hope.

One of the most discouraging days of my pastoral career was the day in 2008 when our church was scheduled to sign a contract to occupy a forty-two-thousand-square-foot facility in a local shopping center. It was going to be our first permanent location and our new ministry headquarters. But at the last minute, one of the tenants chose to exercise a clause in the lease to deny us occupancy.

 RT Timid prayers are a misappropriation of our authority in Christ. #sunstandstill

---

The thing is, we still felt that occupying this facility was God's will for our church.

So we prayed. Not like beggars. Like juggernauts. We got down on our knees on the oil-stained loading docks behind the building and asked God to give us that property.

And do you know what? By September 2009 we were conducting worship services with thousands of people *in that building.* God came through for us, against all odds.

When it comes to standing on God's purposes and promises, why *shouldn't* we push the limits and aggressively pursue new territory?

Prayer is the arena where our faith meets God's abilities. And there is never going to be a moment when the audacity of our faith surpasses God's capacity to respond. That's why timid prayers are a waste of time. And they are a misappropriation of our authority as believers in Christ.

It may take some adjustment to get to a place where extraordinary prayers become ordinary in our lives. It may require that we flex some muscles we didn't know we had. But the Bible leaves us without excuse. We're strong in the Lord. And it's time to put those muscles to work.

PRAYER FOCUS: What is an area where God is calling you to something big? Pray about it today like the juggernaut He made you to be.

Build a Case

Summon your power, O God;
show us your strength, O God, as you have done
before.

—Psalm 68:28

Today's Bible reading: Psalm 68:1–35

Joshua prayed that the sun would stand still because God had promised the Israelites that He would fight for them and defeat their enemies. Joshua's bold request was based on a promise God had made to him (Joshua 10:8).

After the Israelites had worshiped the golden calf and God was threatening to destroy them, Moses found the courage to respond by reminding Him of a promise He had made to Abraham, Isaac, and Jacob (Exodus 32:13).

In today's Bible reading, David spends the first half of Psalm 68 praising God for His past deeds of deliverance and salvation. Then he asks God to show His strength "as you have done before."

In each of these scenarios, one of God's servants is reminding God of something He did in the past or a promise He made concerning the future. What's the reason for this? Did God forget? Does He need an administrative assistant?

Reminding God of His promises isn't about giving Him new information. It's about experiencing His transformation. By going back to the Word of God and recalling His promises and the pattern of His actions in the past, your boldness is stirred. Your desires are aligned with God's purposes. The promises of God are integrated into the fabric of your faith. And your motivations become the same as His motivations.

 RT Reminding God of His promises isn't about giving Him new information. It's about experiencing His transformation. #sunstandstill

---

Think of it as building a case before God.

Now, the first time I heard the phrase *build a case before God,* I didn't get it. It sounded like courtroom theology. It even seemed to have a manipulative vibe. I assure you, however, that building a case before God is biblical. It's practical. And I've seen it transform the prayer lives of thousands of Christians who are tired of praying to God about the same old things in the same old way.

By building a case before God, you can approach Him with audacious faith, because your prayer is based on a solid foundation.

Let's say you have a shortage of money, and you desperately need God to provide for your family. Instead of going to God and pleading with Him on the basis of *pretty please,* go to Him and say,

"Lord, I'm low on resources. One time I read in Matthew 14 how You fed over five thousand people with five loaves and two fish. God, would You multiply that same kind of provision for my family right now?"

It's remarkable to realize that you can pray this way about anything—healing, the salvation of the lost, reconciliation within torn-apart families, depression, children who have wandered, or whatever you're dealing with—at any time. You can pray like this about any area where you're believing God for the impossible. And He has promised to respond.

PRAYER FOCUS: Identify an area where you're desperate for the help of God, find a legitimate rationale in the Bible for why God would want to answer with a yes, then build your case before Him.

Standing Alone

[Joseph's] brothers said to him, "Do you intend to reign over us? Will you actually rule us?" And they hated him all the more because of his dream and what he had said.

—GENESIS 37:8

Today's Bible reading: Genesis 37:2–11

Talk about audacious!

Joseph calls a family meeting one day, skips the small talk, and drops the news. "Just so you know, I'm taking over around here. One day you'll all bow down to me." And in case anyone is prone to argue with his assessment, he throws down the God card, explaining that this play call came directly from heaven.

Joseph's bold vision turns his family against him. Instead of embracing Joseph's destiny, they talk about killing him. Then they sell him into slavery. Years later Joseph's obedience results in false accusations, wrongful imprisonment, and, worst of all, deep isolation and betrayal. His vision doesn't fully come to pass until thirteen years of loneliness and pain have gone by.

Yet Scripture insists that the Lord is with him through it all.

And eventually Joseph rises to become second in command of Egypt and to play a redemptive role in Israel's future.

Divine vision creates division. Or to put it another way, revelation brings isolation. Sometimes no one is going to fully understand what God is doing inside you. And you're left all alone.

 RT Divine vision creates division.
#sunstandstill

At some point your audacious vision may get you beat down. And sold out. And left alone. Hopefully not to the extent of Joseph's experience. Few of us will ever experience physical abuse and solitary confinement for the cause of Christ. But often the hardest pain to deal with is the type you can't see, originating in places you can't reach, resulting in symptoms you can't completely describe.

I've seen wives embrace an audacious vision to bring their marriages under the lordship of Christ. But it was almost impossible for them not to second-guess God's voice when their husbands actually became more resistant in the months that followed rather than running to the altar to repent.

When I was sixteen and began to share my life's vision with my friends, many of them effectively disinvited me from the cool-kid parties. Some of them said they wanted "the old Steven back." That was the one thing I couldn't give them. I was a new person with a new leader, and there was no turning around, regardless of where the crowd would call me.

Whether your vision is met with cheers or jeers, outside opinion cannot be your sustenance. Man cannot live by bread alone, and he certainly can't survive on a steady diet of attaboys. He who lives by the approval of others will die by the absence of the same.

Don't let anybody but God Himself put you in your place. And don't stop forging forward when you encounter opposition. The fact that you're fighting big battles means that you're close to even bigger blessings. The reason you're facing fierce resistance now is that God is preparing an astonishing reward in your future.

But in the meantime, know that there may be stretches where, as the old hymn says, none will go with you. Still, you must follow the One who is with you always.

PRAYER FOCUS: Ask God to prepare you for whatever rejection or abandonment you may have to face today or in the future as you pursue the vision He has for you.

Why Bother?

The devil took [Jesus] to a very high mountain and showed him all the kingdoms of the world and their splendor. "All this I will give you," he said, "if you will bow down and worship me."

—MATTHEW 4:8–9

Today's Bible reading: Matthew 4:1–11

"Everything is possible for him who believes" (Mark 9:23). That's the spirit of a Sun Stand Still faith. Dream. Dare. Do.

But for most of us, there's also a contradictory voice that speaks inside our minds. It's the spirit of discouragement. The spirit of "Take the easy way out and call it a day."

It's the spirit of *Why bother?*

Before Jesus's mission on earth was officially birthed, Satan tried to abort it by offering Him what He came for—glory in all the world—without having to make a stop at a bloody cross along the way. Jesus's commitment to His mission was much too strong to allow Him to consider this option. But sometimes our commitment isn't so strong.

You and I are faced with diversions and discouragements all

the time. When God says to us, "It's possible," the enemy is right there alongside saying a little louder, "Why bother?" And it's appealing too. Doesn't it make more sense just to settle for what's easier?

When you start believing God's promises in a bold way, the enemy's first line of defense is to hit Play on this sentiment of apathy in your spirit and put it on repeat, *Why bother?...Why bother?... Why bother?...*

 RT When God says to us, "It's possible," the enemy is right there alongside saying a little louder, "Why bother?" #sunstandstill

---

I've known people who have had hopeless feelings about their commitment to spend time with God every day. *Why bother reading my Bible today?* they think. *I know I'm not going to read it tomorrow, because I always fall off the wagon.*

Some people feel the same way about their jobs. *Why should I bother to do my best? I don't get paid all that much, and nobody appreciates what I do anyway.*

I see teenagers all the time who give up their virginity because they think, *Why bother being pure when nobody around me seems to hold to that standard?*

The enemy is always going to say "Why bother?" anytime God says "It's possible." And this is the place where dreams die and faith fails for so many people.

But that doesn't have to be you. You can choose what you're

going to listen to, whether it's the cheers coming from God or the jeers coming from your enemy. Tune in to the right voice so that what God wants to do in your life will not be hindered. Give your miracle a chance to make it to the finish line.

PRAYER FOCUS: Pray for God's help to recognize the enemy's voice of discouragement or distraction for what it is—and then tune it out.

Dress for the Wedding

*"You do not want to leave too, do you?" Jesus asked
the Twelve.*

*Simon Peter answered him, "Lord, to whom shall
we go? You have the words of eternal life."*

—John 6:67–68

Today's Bible reading: John 6:60–69

Let me see if you can relate to a scenario.

You're dressed to the nines and looking fresh for a formal
event—let's say it's a wedding—and you're driving there in your
car. Along the way you have to stop for some gas.

As you're pumping gas, you realize, *I am completely overdressed
for this occasion. Here I am in a suit and tie (or dress and heels), pumping
gas.* You almost feel like you need to explain to the people around
you who are rocking shorts and flip-flops. "Hey, don't mind me.
I'm just stopping by. Headed to a wedding, you know."

Can you recall an awkward situation like that in your life? I
totally can.

And I can also recall times when God has placed visions inside me and I have felt as if I was "overdressed" for the place where I was on the way to where God was taking me.

It was 2006, and our church was about two months old. The day before Easter we had a huge event. As a part of it, we rented a helicopter and used it to drop thousands of plastic Easter eggs onto a football field. Inside some of the eggs were tickets redeemable for prizes like Wii systems and Xboxes. The two thousand people who were there that day loved it.

On Easter morning I stood in front of our church of about two hundred people and said, "Wasn't it amazing to have two thousand people at our Easter event yesterday?!"

Everybody cheered.

So then I was like, "What are we gonna do next Easter when we have two thousand people coming to church every Sunday?"

Crickets.

Nobody cheered. Nobody said "Amen."

 RT If you want to be victorious, sometimes you have to be willing to look ridiculous. #sunstandstill

---

It was awkward. I'm going for it, proclaiming to our little church that we're going to have two thousand people. And the two hundred people who are sitting there look at me like, "Yeah, well, we'll see." Not even the staff was saying "Amen." Now that I think of it, I should have fired somebody.

When you're praying for the sun to stand still, there are going to be times when *you* get it but others aren't nearly so sure.

I think that may be the same tension Jesus and His disciples are experiencing after Jesus gives His sermon about eating His flesh and drinking His blood (John 6:25–59). A bunch of Jesus's fair-weather followers head for the door.

"You don't want to leave too, do you?" Jesus asks the disciples.

Crickets.

But then Peter speaks up with the confession I love: "Lord, to whom shall we go? You have the words of eternal life."

The Twelve may momentarily feel like an abandoned bunch of losers, but when it comes down to it, they are dressed for the occasion. For the Kingdom that is already in the making but not yet fully manifest.

The fact is, everybody around you isn't always going to understand what God has put inside you. And that's okay. If you want to be victorious, sometimes you have to be willing to look ridiculous. But when you get to where God is taking you, they won't be laughing at you anymore. I can testify. The whole church was cheering a year later when I announced our Easter Sunday attendance: 2,058 people.

You're not staying at the gas station. You're headed to the wedding.

And when you get where God is taking you, you'll be glad you dressed for the occasion.

PRAYER FOCUS: Pray for the ability to be faithful today in an area of your life where God may be calling you to look ridiculous.

God Is Great

The Lord is the everlasting God,
the Creator of the ends of the earth.
He will not grow tired or weary,
and his understanding no one can fathom.

—Isaiah 40:28

Today's Bible reading: Isaiah 40:12–28

When my son Elijah was five years old, he came to me one day when I was at home working out, and he told me he wanted me to bring his pirate ship downstairs. From his limited perspective, absolutely nothing was more important in that moment than the safe and immediate transportation of this toy pirate ship. To me, the need wasn't quite so urgent. I tried to blow him off. He tried to wear me down. I didn't budge. Neither did he. Finally he tried a different angle: "Daddy, I really need my pirate ship. Do you think you're strong enough to do that for me?"

Smart kid. When all else fails, appeal to Daddy's pride. Elijah got his pirate ship. I got a lesson about how God sees the needs of His children. He likes to show off His strength and display His power. He doesn't do it to protect His pride. It's all about demonstrating His glory.

If your problem is too big for you, it's just the right size for God. He's strong enough to do that for you, whatever your "that" may be.

Isaiah 40 is only one of tons of Bible passages I could point you to that extol the greatness of God—because His greatness is the theme of the Scriptures, from beginning to end. He's eternal. He's almighty. He's all-knowing. Why would you strain and stumble beneath a load that's too heavy when you have a God like this as your Father?

 RT If your problem is too big for you, it's just the right size for God. #sunstandstill

---

When we see God for who He is, our small dreams are eclipsed by His unlimited strength as it becomes increasingly clear there is nothing our Father in heaven cannot accomplish.

And because God is so great, no prayer of faith to God is a waste of time. The measure of God's abilities will always surpass the measure of our audacity. No prayer is too big for our God. No vision too sweeping. No risk too great. God has never been nervous about His ability to live up to our faith in Him. And we are invited to believe Him for the kinds of things most people would consider outside the realm of possibility.

If there is no limit to what God can do, then there is also no limit to what we can dream or pray or accomplish in His service.

The God of the Bible can do whatever He pleases. And what pleases Him is to show off His power for His glory and renown. So give Him the opportunity.

Dream God-worthy dreams.

Pray faith-fueled prayers.

Live a life that is explainable only by the existence of a God who is infinitely great.

PRAYER FOCUS: Spend time today praising God for His greatness— His unlimited power, knowledge, and glory.

God Is Good

Praise the LORD, O my soul,
and forget not all his benefits—
who forgives all your sins
and heals all your diseases,
who redeems your life from the pit
and crowns you with love and compassion.

—PSALM 103:2–4

Today's Bible reading: Psalm 103:1–22

It's one thing to acknowledge that God is great, as we did in yesterday's devotional. Most major world religions recognize that much about their respective deities. What sets the Christian faith apart is an unrelenting hope in the fact that God is good. That fact was settled once and for all on the Cross. And it's really good news. After all, what good is infinite power if you have no access to it? Yes, God does whatever He desires. Thankfully, what He desires is to make His power and resources available to you, and He wants them to pour forth in abundance from your life.

God's goodness means that all of His greatness is intended to work in your life *for your good.* Not necessarily your momentary happiness. But your ultimate good. Romans 8:28 says, "We know that in *all* things *God works* for the *good* of those who love him, who have been called according to his purpose." That isn't a statement of probability. It's a revelation of the unchanging character of God. *Good* describes what God has been, is, and will always be doing.

The survival of your audacity depends on your knowing deep down that your God is good. The problem is, pain and struggle can color the lens through which we view God's activity in our lives. We can easily lose track of the truth. And in that state of emotional haze, it won't be long before the goodness of God begins to seem like a lie.

 RT Whatever your past performance or present struggle, God is with you to help, save, and heal. #sunstandstill

---

But look back over your life and remember. No matter what you've been through or are going through, God has been good to you. You're here. You're alive. You're breathing. He has let you see another day. And He has brought you to today's devotional time with a sincere desire for you to experience more of Him.

He has been good to you.

And when you remember that fact, it changes the way you see your challenges.

That's what David is doing in Psalm 103. He could focus on his failures. Instead, he remembers and focuses on God's forgiveness. He could focus on his diseases. Instead, he remembers and focuses on how God has been able to heal them. He could focus on the pain of the pit. Instead, he remembers and focuses on the fact that God has pulled him out of it.

Difficulties are going to come. Walking with God sometimes means walking through trials. But instead of focusing on your situation, remember God's goodness. Let it permeate your thoughts and emotions in your quiet time with God today. Because whatever your past performance or present struggle, God is with you to help, save, and heal.

He will, because He is a good God.

PRAYER FOCUS: Spend time today remembering God's goodness in your life and thanking Him for it.

The God Who Provides

Abraham looked up and there in a thicket he saw a ram
caught by its horns. He went over and took the ram
and sacrificed it as a burnt offering instead of his son.
So Abraham called that place The Lord Will Provide.

—Genesis 22:13–14

Today's Bible reading: Genesis 22:1–18

At our website (sunstandstill.org) we ask people to submit their "impossible" needs so our prayer team can lift them up. One day I thought it would be interesting to find out what the number-one area of need is. Do you know what I discovered? Most people are asking for some kind of material provision from God.

People are saying things like…

"My hours were cut in half. And I know that if I go to my boss and complain, he'll find somebody else to do my work."

"We were planning on retiring three and a half years from now. But now our investments are worth less than they were a few years ago."

"We lost our health insurance, and the next month our child had to go to the hospital. Now we've got all these bills."

Some would accuse these people of somehow being unspir-
itual for seeking God in the area of material provision. Listen, God
provides in all kinds of ways. He provides intangibles like joy and
hope and peace, and these are invaluable. But the Bible shows us
over and over again, without apology, that He also provides in the
most tangible areas of a person's life.

One day God instructs Abraham to take his young son to a
mountain and sacrifice him on an altar. If God asked me to do
the same thing to one of my sons, I'm afraid it would be the end of
the line in my journey of obedience. I couldn't fathom following
through with a command like this. But apparently Abraham has
more faith than I do. He doesn't know exactly how God is going to
turn this one around, but after his long life of seeing God act, he
declares, "God himself will provide the lamb" (verse 8).

 RT Before you get to the peak of provision, you must be
found faithful in the valley of decision. #sunstandstill

Just as Abraham is about to plunge the knife into Isaac, the
Lord intervenes to stop him, explaining that Abraham has passed
the test.

Immediately there it is: a ram caught in a thicket. This is the
material provision Abraham has been yearning for—much more
than anybody ever wanted employment, a secure retirement, or
money for hospital bills. God has made a way to save the life of his
son. On the spot Abraham names the hill where he is standing
Yahweh Yireh, or "The Lord Will Provide."

There will never be a shortage in God's supply. There might only be a shortage in our capacity to believe Him.

God has blessed me materially many times. I call these "peaks of provision." But do you know what I've figured out? Before every peak of provision, there's a valley of decision. Like Abraham, each of us has to decide if we'll trust God and follow what He's telling us.

Maybe right now you're stuck in your life because God has you in the valley of decision. If you'll walk through the valley and obey Him—no matter how hard it seems right now—He will bring you to a peak on the other side. Before you get to the peak of provision, you must be found faithful in the valley of decision.

When you get to the mountain, you'll be able to look back to the place God brought you from and say, "The Lord has provided." And you'll be able to worship Him as the all-sufficient God.

PRAYER FOCUS: If you're in need of provision from God, ask His help to trust Him more in the valley of decision where you find yourself today.

The Chariots and Horsemen of Israel

The LORD opened the servant's eyes, and he looked
and saw the hills full of horses and chariots of fire
all around Elisha.

—2 KINGS 6:17

Today's Bible reading: 2 Kings 6:8–23

In today's Scripture passage, the prophet Elisha has just been doing his prophetic thing—passing on insights from God for the good of his nation—and it has him caught up in the crosscurrents of a military conflict. An enemy army has surrounded the city where Elisha is staying, solely to take the prophet out. Permanently.

Here's the thing. Elisha is so full of faith that he has the ability to see God's angelic army. Earlier in his ministry Elisha had exclaimed, "The chariots and horsemen of Israel!" when he had seen Elijah taken up to heaven (2 Kings 2:11–12). And now, years later, Elisha is seeing the heavenly chariots and horsemen again. The angels are lined up to fight on Israel's side.

But Elisha's servant doesn't have the same kind of faith and can't see the spectacular scene.

So Elisha prays, "O Lord, open his eyes so he may see" (2 Kings 6:17).

And there before the servant's eyes, they appear: rank upon rank of the angelic host, shining with heaven's own light. They are there to protect Elisha, the man of God.

That's what faith does.

Faith opens our eyes so that we might see the God who is already at work on our behalf. Faith opens our eyes to the fact that there is a God who is fighting for us, a God who is faithful to us, a God who will make a way for us.

One of the people who has written in to our website (sun standstill.org) is a woman named Kimberly. She had an incredible story to share.

 RT Faith opens our eyes so that we might see the God who is already at work on our behalf. #sunstandstill

---

Things had been going very badly for Kimberly. Her father died of a drug overdose. Her fiancé overdosed on pain medication, though he survived. Kimberly had a car accident because she was using drugs, and this led to her children being taken away from her. She lost her home and at one point found herself sleeping in some bushes.

At this point God seemed as far away from her as He possibly could be.

Faith didn't open her eyes so much as it opened her ears.

One morning she woke up with the definite impression that someone was talking to her. "What is keeping you from Me?" a voice asked. Kimberly looked around. No one was there.

What is keeping you from Me?

That was the beginning of Kimberly's road to God. Since that date she's never used again. She's in drug recovery, is married, and has her children back. She wrote to say that she has a Page 23 vision and is pursuing it.

"How awesome is the God we serve!" she wrote to me.

Sometimes we hear about blind faith. But the truth is, audacious faith is anything but blind.

PRAYER FOCUS: Ask God to open your eyes to what He's already doing in your life as you exercise your faith.

Your Faith, God's Faithfulness

If we are faithless,
he will remain faithful,
for he cannot disown himself.

—2 TIMOTHY 2:13

Today's Bible reading: 2 Timothy 2:1–13

I don't think we can ever talk enough about the faithfulness of God. It's the starting place of any big prayer or act of faith.

Our faith may fail. But God's faithfulness never will. Our faith is not built on the fault line of feelings or the flood plain of our performance. We build our faith on solid ground. Higher ground. We build on the faithfulness of God. That's what 2 Timothy 2:13 tells us.

Faithfulness is not merely some general attribute of God's, but rather it extends to the workings of your life. A faithful God has allowed you to breathe every breath you've ever breathed. His faithfulness has permitted you to experience the highest mountaintops of your life. His faithfulness has enabled you to endure the darkest valleys.

So today, if your faith is low because of a shortage of resources or because of a relational tension or because of an emotional depression or because of anything else, that's okay. Your faith isn't in your faith. Your faith is in your God.

But I also believe there's another side to all this that we can't afford to ignore. God is faithful even if we are faithless. But God shows His faithfulness in a special way toward those who show their faith in Him.

I'm not talking out of both sides of my mouth. It's simple, really. God is always faithful. But the people who step out in faith have the opportunity to see God come through for them and move in ways that those who are faithless don't have.

 RT God shows His faithfulness in a special way to those who show their faith in Him. #sunstandstill

---

God would have remained faithful if Moses had remained in the desert, herding sheep. But because Moses had the faith to be God's representative before Pharaoh, he had a front-row seat to the ten plagues and the parting of the Red Sea—both of them huge demonstrations of God's faithfulness.

God would have remained faithful if Daniel hadn't had the courage to keep praying to God when he was told not to. But because Daniel had the faith to persist, he had the privilege of proving God's faithfulness in the lions' den.

God would have remained faithful if Peter hadn't walked on water. But because Peter had the faith to step out of the boat, he saw Jesus's faithfulness in a way the other disciples didn't.

Maybe we could sum it up like this: God has demonstrated His past faithfulness to give us a foundation for our faith. Now, if you'll show God your faith, He'll show you His faithfulness. Not because you have earned it, but because you have put yourself in a position to see it.

PRAYER FOCUS: Declare your faith to God, and ask Him to reveal His faithfulness to you today in a bold and tangible way.

Keep Swinging

Our struggle is not against flesh and blood, but against the...powers of this dark world and against the spiritual forces of evil in the heavenly realms.

—Ephesians 6:12

Today's Bible reading: Ephesians 6:10–18

An older pastor used to tell me, "Remember, son, serving God is not a playground. It's a battleground."

When we're trying to live out our audacious faith, we have to expect some opposition and some adversity along the way. And although it may appear that the obstacle standing in our way is simply an obstructive person or an inconvenient fact about the world, there is also an unseen, spiritually multilayered reality to what is going on.

Maybe that's not what you want to hear. Verily I say unto you, I don't like it much either. But that's the way it is.

We need to expect moments of crisis and struggle. We need to get ready to fight. And we need to hold on to our hope for the final victory. Because our conflict sets the stage for God's conquest. Resistance is often fiercest on the borderline of a breakthrough.

If you never faced an enemy of God, you would never experience God's victory. Where there is no opposition, there is no opportunity.

But don't we typically think of adversity as the opposite of opportunity? I usually pray for God to *remove* all the obstacles and opposition in my life. Adversity gets in the way of opportunity, to my way of thinking.

God, though, doesn't think like I think. Instead of taking away our adversity, He develops our faith and demonstrates His strength by working through our adversity.

 RT Where there is no opposition, there is no opportunity. #sunstandstill

---

I'm not suggesting that you pick a fight with the devil. I'm not advising you to invite pain and suffering into your life. And you won't have to. Adversity is inevitable. I'm simply saying that when the battle begins, you have two options. You can stand there and get beaten to a bloody pulp, abandon your faith, and curse the day you were born. Or you can seize the opportunity to experience God's power and goodness in a new way, watching in awe as He fights for you.

Throw the first punch. Seize the opportunity to see God fight for you rather than let your adversary destroy you blow by blow.

And don't stop swinging. Don't give up. Don't resign your faith the first time things don't go your way. Or even if certain things never go your way.

I don't know what kinds of enemies you will have to engage as you fight the fight of audacious faith today. You may have to demonstrate the patience of Job and the compassion of Christ toward a rebellious teenager. You may have to press through chronic physical pain, wondering why God has healed so many other people but hasn't healed you.

Maybe you think I can't relate to your particular level of hardship. And you may be right. But I've had a ringside seat to watch some godly people go all fifteen rounds with crippling circumstances. And they were still standing strong in faith at the end.

You can be too.

PRAYER FOCUS: Ask God to show you which battles to engage in and how you can fight them in His almighty strength.

Faith Confessions

From now on we regard no one from a worldly point of view.... If anyone is in Christ, he is a new creation; the old has gone, the new has come!

—2 CORINTHIANS 5:16–17

Today's Bible reading: 2 Corinthians 5:11–21

In an earlier devotional I wrote about the importance of speaking the Word to yourself. One of the tools we developed to help with this is the 12 Audacious Faith Confessions. It's based on the simple idea that we're changed people once we trust Christ. We're a "new creation," as Paul says. We only need to activate our new identity.

The faith confessions aren't magical. They aren't exactly mantras. But they *are* declarations of truth based solidly in the Bible. Therefore, they have power in them. God's Word does not return void.

After I introduced these faith confessions to our church, inspiring stories started flooding in. Here's one example.

A teenager wrote to me about how she had been cutting herself in the bathroom at school because she felt ugly and unwanted. But she had started to renew her mind each day, several times a day, by speaking, "I have no insecurity, because I see myself the way God sees me." As she did so, the need to dull the edge of her self-loathing mind-set gradually subsided.

Others wrote in to tell about victories that, while perhaps not as physically noticeable as this teenager's, are every bit as significant.

 RT I act in audacious faith to change the world in my generation. #sunstandstill

---

How much difference will it make in your life if you preach the following realities to yourself every day?

1. I am fully forgiven and free from all shame and condem- nation (Romans 8:1–2; Ephesians 1:7–8; 1 John 1:9).
2. I act in audacious faith to change the world in my genera- tion (Joshua 10:12–14; John 14:12).
3. I have no fear or anxiety; I trust in the Lord with all my heart (Proverbs 3:5–6; Philippians 4:6–7; 1 Peter 5:7).
4. I am able to fulfill the calling God has placed on my life (Exodus 3:9–12; Psalm 57:2; Colossians 1:24–29).
5. I am fully resourced to do everything God has called me to do (Deuteronomy 8:18; Luke 6:38; Philippians 4:13).
6. I have no insecurity, because I see myself the way God sees me (Genesis 1:26–27; Psalm 139:13–16; Ephesians 5:25–27).

7. I am a faithful spouse and a godly parent—our family is blessed (Deuteronomy 6:6–9; Ephesians 5:22–25; Colossians 3:18–19; 1 Peter 3:1–7). [Note: If you're single, you might want to slip in "future" before "faithful spouse."]

8. I am completely whole—physically, mentally, and emotionally (Psalm 103:1–5; Matthew 8:16–17; 2 Corinthians 5:17; 1 Peter 2:24).

9. I am increasing in influence and favor for the kingdom of God (Genesis 45:4–8; 1 Samuel 2:26; Acts 2:37–47).

10. I am enabled to walk in the sacrificial love of Christ (2 Thessalonians 2:16–17; 1 John 3:16; 4:9–12).

11. I have the wisdom of the Lord concerning every decision I make (2 Chronicles 1:7–12; Proverbs 2:6; Ecclesiastes 2:26; James 1:5).

12. I am protected from all harm and evil in Jesus's name (Genesis 50:20; Psalm 3:1–3; 2 Thessalonians 3:2–3).

When you preach to yourself like this, it creates a context for your faith to grow. It accelerates the process of putting away the "old man" or "old woman" you were. You are being transformed into Christ's likeness with ever-increasing glory (2 Corinthians 3:18).

As simple as it may seem, integrating these faith confessions into your daily habits could instigate incredible change in your life.

PRAYER FOCUS: Pray about one or more of the faith confessions where you need God to change your heart so you can affirm these confessions in all confidence.

Small Beginning to Big Finish

I tell you the truth, if you have faith as small as a mustard seed, you can say to this mountain, "Move from here to there" and it will move. Nothing will be impossible for you.

—MATTHEW 17:20

Today's Bible reading: Matthew 17:14–21

The situation around you may look nothing like the vision God has put inside you. But by the power of faith, God can turn your small beginning into a grand finale. That's the miracle of the mustard seed.

The tiniest level of faith, applied and exerted consistently over the course of time, can move the biggest mountain in your life. Having the faith to start small in the face of the most overwhelming odds is about as audacious as it gets.

Holly and I made two financial promises to each other when we got married. We committed to always put God first by giving at least 10 percent of all our income back to Him. And we committed to staying completely free of consumer debt. We wanted to get in a position to write our largest check each month to the local church, not the mortgage company.

When we started giving 10 percent of our income away, it didn't seem like much. But every year we have raised that percentage and have given away more. And do you know what? When we were looking at our records at the end of last year, we honestly couldn't believe how much money we had been able to give to our church. The amount we gave away in that one year far exceeded our total household income in the first year of our marriage.

It didn't get that way overnight. We took small steps toward our big dream of radical generosity. And although we still have a lot of room to grow, God has fulfilled His promise to make His resources overflow in our lives.

 RT Stop waiting for what you want. Work with what you have. #sunstandstill

This may seem like a small, isolated example to you. But that's the point. I'm trying to get you to see that you need to build on small successes if you're going to fully realize your God-sized vision. And of course this doesn't apply just to finances.

Let's say you have a strained relationship with your teenage daughter and your Sun Stand Still prayer is that God will bring your family into harmony. Start small with that. Before you go to sleep tonight, find one positive thing you can verbally affirm in the life of your child. I doubt she'll respond right away by hugging you and filling you in on the darkest secrets of her life. But a seed will be planted. And whether you see it or not, God will start to water that seed.

If you continue to plant seeds, there may come a day when you see signs of life springing up all around you. But it doesn't start with a harvest. It starts with a seed that initiates a process.

Most dreams die in the womb of small beginnings. Don't let that be true for you.

Stop waiting for what you want. Work with what you have.

There's no better time to begin than today.

PRAYER FOCUS: Ask God to show you what you have to start with and to help you stick with the process.

In the Middle of a Move of God

I heard the voice of the Lord saying, "Whom shall
I send? And who will go for us?"
And I said, "Here am I. Send me!"

—Isaiah 6:8

Today's Bible reading: Isaiah 6:1–8

Do you want to know how it feels to see God accomplish the impossible right in front of your eyes? God is inviting you to be a supporting character in His story as it's playing out today. He is casting you in the thick of the plot.

See, when you begin to activate your faith and pray Sun Stand Still prayers, you're doing more than just changing *your* life. You're placing yourself in the middle of a move of God.

You're participating in a mission to manifest the kingdom of God in every sphere of your influence. You're responding to God's call to Christians everywhere to embrace, harness, and ultimately shape their culture. And together we are a powerful force.

Our message—all about forgiveness and grace in Jesus Christ—

is the most relevant message in the history of the world. We can't be timid about it.

We know what we believe, we know why we believe it, and we're determined to live it out with all our hearts. We're not perfect, but our passion is sincere. We're not here merely to survive or to condemn the world but to transform it for the glory of God. And we're here to stay.

We're the living, breathing, forcefully advancing people of God. We are a generation of Joshuas.

I'm sure you're asking yourself, *Am I really ready to take my place in the middle of a move of God?*

I believe you are. I believe God has been preparing you for this all your life.

What it takes now is simply willingness.

Joshua was willing to act in audacious faith once God had stiffened his backbone with the command "Be strong and courageous" (Joshua 1:6, 9). This is what led to that insane yet inspired prayer for the sun and moon to halt in the sky.

 RT We're not here merely to survive or to condemn the world but to transform it for the glory of God. And we're here to stay. #sunstandstill

---

Moses, Elisha, Paul, Peter, and others we've studied in these devotionals were willing too.

There's another biblical character who shows us the spirit of willingness as plain as any.

Granted a vision of God's holiness, Isaiah is filled with eagerness to do whatever God wants him to do. Here's Isaiah's Page 23 vision: to speak on the Lord's behalf to the rebellious nation of Israel. This is hardly an easy task to contemplate. Yet Isaiah is like a schoolboy with the right answer, waving his arm and calling out to the teacher, "Me! Me! Me!"

"Here am I. Send me!" Isaiah pleads to God.

Does that kind of eagerness to fulfill God's call upon you characterize your spirit today?

You don't have to fully understand. You only have to be willing to follow, and the adventure will begin. God will do the miraculous, and you're along for the ride.

When Jesus was birthed into this world, an angel said, "Nothing is impossible with God" (Luke 1:37).

When we are birthed into our roles in God's movement in the world, we must say the same thing. Nothing is impossible with God. *Nothing.*

Go out in audacious faith.

PRAYER FOCUS: Pray to God about living a lifestyle from now on that expects the sun to stand still over and over again as God chooses to act. Tell Him, "Send me!"

ABOUT THE AUTHORS

STEVEN FURTICK is the founder and lead pastor of Elevation Church based in Charlotte, North Carolina. He is also the *New York Times* best-selling author of *Greater* and *Sun Stand Still*. Pastor Steven holds a master of divinity degree from the Southern Baptist Theological Seminary. He and his wife, Holly, live in the Charlotte area with their two sons, Elijah and Graham, and daughter, Abbey.

ERIC STANFORD is a writer and editor living in Colorado Springs, Colorado. Along with his wife, Elisa, he runs Edit Resource, LLC (editresource.com). They have two children: Eden and Elizabeth.

Also Available

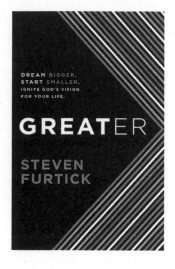

If you sense that you were meant for more but feel stuck where you are, *Greater* will give you the confidence to know that nothing is impossible with God, the clarity to see the next step He's calling you to take, and the courage to do anything He tells you to do.

Sun Stand Still is about believing God can do impossible things through you and acting on that astonishing truth. Come discover what can happen when you dare to ask God for the impossible.

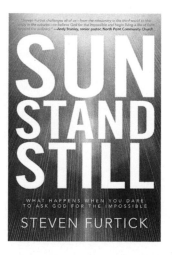